SOMALIA OPERATIONS:
Lessons Learned

SOMALIA OPERATIONS: Lessons Learned

Kenneth Allard

National Defense University Press
Ft. McNair, Washington, DC

National Defense University Press Publications

To increase general knowledge and inform discussion, the Institute for National Strategic Studies, through its publication arm the NDU Press, publishes McNair Papers; proceedings of University- and Institute-sponsored symposia; books relating to U.S. national security, especially to issues of joint, combined, or coalition warfare, peacekeeping operations, and national strategy; and a variety of briefer works designed to circulate contemporary comment and offer alternatives to current policy. The Press occasionally publishes out-of-print defense classics, historical works, and other especially timely or distinguished writing on national security.

NDU Press publications are sold by the U.S. Government Printing Office. For ordering information, call (202) 512-1800, or write to the Superintendent of Documents, U.S. Government Printing Office, Washington, DC 20402.

First printing, January 1995

For sale by the U.S. Government Printing Office
Superintendent of Documents, Mail Stop: SSOP
Washington, DC 20402-9328
ISBN 0-16-045577-4

Dedication

This book is respectfully dedicated to the memories of Master Sergeant Gary I. Gordon and Sergeant First Class Randall D. Shughart, United States Army, who were killed in action on October 3, 1993 in Mogadishu, Somalia. For "conspicuous gallantry and intrepidity at the risk of life above and beyond the call of duty" while defending their embattled Task Force Ranger comrades, these soldiers were posthumously awarded the Medal of Honor on May 23, 1994.

Greater love hath no man than this,
that a man lay down his life for his friends.
John 15:13

Contents

Foreword

The American mission in Somalia presented U.S. forces with a variety of difficult operational challenges as they tried to bring peace to a country ravaged by natural and man-made disasters. After initial success in the summer of 1992 in restoring order and saving thousands of lives, American soldiers clashed with Somali forces and were withdrawn in the spring of 1994. In the months that followed, we have studied what the Somalia experience can teach us about peace missions and learned how we might improve our capabilities across the spectrum of joint operations.

This book represents the first time a new tool—the Joint Universal Lessons Learned System—is being used to evaluate an operation in its totality. With it, Colonel Kenneth Allard assesses the operation from its early stages of humanitarian relief through the de facto combat of peace enforcement. He has organized the lessons learned for ease of reading and enlivened them with numerous concrete and anecdotal examples. Although focused on the operational level, the insights of this study should be of interest to strategists and policymakers as well.

Lessons are only truly learned when we incorporate them into our planning, doctrine, tactics, and training—a process which can take some time. The author has taken the essential first step by identifying and articulating the hard lessons of Somalia with candor and objectivity. But even as we resolve not to repeat mistakes, we should not allow the tragic events in the latter stages of our Somalia operations to obscure the many things we did right. These too are lessons, ones to build upon as we prepare to meet further challenges in the complex world of peace operations.

ERVIN J. ROKKE
Lieutentant General, U.S. Air Force
President, National Defense University

Acknowledgments

This study reflects in large measure the active sponsorship and encouragement of Major General Stephen Silvasy, Jr., USA, Director for Operational Plans & Interoperability (J-7) of the Joint Staff. Grateful thanks are extended to him and his staff.

At National Defense University, similar thanks are due to the Director of the Institute for National Strategic Studies (INSS), Dr. Hans Binnendijk, and Major General John Sewall, USA (Ret.) for their leadership and support for this project. Lieutenant Colonel Susan Flores, USMC, and Dr. William Lewis, both of INSS, provided indispensable help by their hard work throughout the project as well as by their many helpful suggestions as the drafts took shape. Dr. Fred Kiley, Director of the National Defense University Press, and his colleague Mr. George Maerz managed all aspects of the publication process with characteristic professionalism. Mr. Don Barry, Mr. Alex Contreras, Ms. Rhonda Gross, and Mr. Juan Medrano of the NDU Graphics Department brought their unique talents to the design of the cover and the illustrations contained in this publication. Ms. Theresa Chapman of the NDU Library and Mr. Jim Peters of *JFQ* provided helpful bibliographic and technical support.

Special thanks are also due to the following people who reviewed the draft and provided many helpful suggestions: Ambassador Robert Oakley;

Lieutenant General Robert B. Johnston, USMC; Lieutenant General Thomas M. Montgomery, USA; Lieutenant General Anthony C. Zinni, USMC; Major General Frank Libutti, USMC; Colonel Carl Farris, Lieutenant Colonel Sam Butler and Professor Kenneth Menkhaus of the U.S. Army Peacekeeping Institute; Colonel F.M. Lorenz, USMC; Colonel Gary Anderson, USMC; Colonel Thomas Leney, USA; Colonel Robert Killebrew, USA; and Lieutenant Colonel(P) Eric T. Olson, USA. Additionally, Mr. Bill Dawson of the U.S. Central Command and Ms. Joani Schaefer of the U.S. Transportation Command provided many useful insights into the key roles played by their respective organizations during the Somalia operations.

While sincere thanks are due all these people, errors of fact and interpretation are, of course, the sole responsibility of the author.

Preface

Multilateral peace operations are an important component of our strategy. From traditional peacekeeping to peace enforcement, multilateral peace operations are sometimes the best way to prevent, contain, or resolve conflicts that could otherwise be far more costly and deadly.

The President's National Security Strategy
July 1994

If today you are a soldier, a sailor, an airman, or a marine, then you know in some very personal ways that the world is a changed and changing place. Far from ushering in an era of peace, our victory in the Cold War was quickly followed by combat in Operations *Just Cause* and *Desert Storm*. And even as our Armed Forces were being reduced from Cold War levels, they were being committed to a new class of military missions, called peace operations, in Somalia, in parts of the former Yugoslavia, and (at this writing) in Haiti.

Peace operations are unique because they are conducted with the increasing involvement of the international community, usually with mandates from the United Nations and sometimes with the United States as the lead partner in coalitions drawn from a number of different nations. These partnerships can create some real challenges on all sides, but there are two important advantages for the United States to keep in mind. First, we clearly benefit when other nations help shoulder the burden. Second, the voice of the international community is important—just look at the impact of world opinion in building the diverse coalition with which we stood during the Gulf War. The bottom line is that our ability to build and support multinational coalitions is now an important part of our national security strategy in the post-Cold War world.

The significance of this strategic turning point has, for the last 2 years, prompted the National Defense University to study peace operations as part of its mission of extensive research and teaching on national security issues; this book is one of the products of that program. With the cooperation of the Joint Staff, a team at the National Defense University's Institute for National Strategic Studies examined reports on U.S. operations in Somalia filed in the Joint Universal Lessons Learned System (JULLS), in an effort to relate them to joint doctrinal principles as well as other research on this subject.[1] The emphasis throughout this effort has been to focus on the most important lessons at the *operational level,* primarily those which might be encountered at the joint task force planning level or at the headquarters of its major force components. Because this level is the one that ties together the strategic and the tactical, some of those lessons are relevant here as well, but to help bound the problem, those insights are usually presented as either causes or effects.

What makes the Somalia experience important

for U.S. Armed Forces is that it was an operation that went through three distinct phases:

- An airlift that provided food relief and medical supplies to a multitude of sick, starving people
- An intervention force that combined continued humanitarian assistance activities with military operations meant to provide better security for relief efforts
- A military force that provided the bulk of the combat power for the first "peace enforcement" operation in the history of the United Nations.

In addition to underlining the complexity of peace operations, these three distinct phases show that, as the level of conflict intensified, some things changed more than others. The specific mission elements examined here also provide a sobering glimpse of the challenges imposed by a country in chaos, where the effects of a harsh natural environment were made even more severe by clan warfare and the absence of government.

As its title implies, this book examines certain operational issues raised by our recent experience in Somalia, especially those involving the teamwork required by joint forces. It is an *initial look* at those operational issues—not a comprehensive history either of U.S. involvement in Somalia or even of the key functional areas it examines. It is best described as a composite after-action review—a preliminary look at the operation's major insights based on the best data currently available. Where relevant, these insights have been compared to more detailed analyses of various phases of the operation, such as those on

UNOSOM II prepared by the Center for Army Lessons Learned at Fort Leavenworth, KS, and the *United States Forces Somalia After Action Report (Montgomery Report)* now being readied for publication by the Army Peacekeeping Institute at the U.S. Army War College.

Because "lessons learned" often tend to reflect what went wrong rather than what went right, it might be possible to think that these operations were less than successful: this is simply not the case. Although they did not carry out the more ambitious goals of U.N.-sponsored nation-building, U.S. forces sent to Somalia clearly *did* execute their missions successfully, relieving untold suffering through humanitarian assistance and executing their military responsibilities with skill and professionalism. In fact, those skills and can-do attitudes were especially important in overcoming the effects of many of the problems cited here. Those who took such initiatives and provided the "work-arounds" should be the first to appreciate the importance of learning from their experiences.

A final caveat is that Somalia was a mission that occurred under unique circumstances. Future operations under different circumstances will likely produce different results. Common sense suggests that the lessons offered here should be balanced against changing mission requirements and conditions. Future missions, however, are likely to contain enough parallels—of failed states and the hardships brought about by natural and man-made disasters—that the lessons learned in Somalia warrant close attention.

NOTE

1. A list of relevant National Defense University publications is at appendix A. Unless otherwise noted, all direct quotations used in this handbook are taken from reports on Somalia operations filed in the Joint Universal Lessons Learned data base.

SOMALIA OPERATIONS:
Lessons Learned

I. THE OPERATIONAL CONTEXT

Peacekeeping isn't a soldier's job, but only a soldier can do it.

Military Sociologist Charles Moskos

The U.N. and Peace Operations

At the end of World War II, the United States helped to found the United Nations and was one of the original signers of the U.N. Charter. Among other provisions, the Charter contains two important sections to help its members "maintain international peace and security." Although the Charter never uses the word, the generic term for these measures is *peacekeeping*, the kinds of observer or truce supervisory missions that occurred after a conflict, when combatants wanted to have the benefit of a trusted third party to act as a buffer. Traditionally, these missions have been known as "Chapter VI actions," because that section of the Charter deals with the peaceful settlement of international disputes. However, Chapter VII contains the term *peace enforcement,* referring to military intervention authorized by the U.N. Security Council— blockades, enforcement of sanctions, forceful disarmament, and direct military action. These categories haven't always fit

3

situations that seemed to go beyond peacekeeping but stopped short of actual combat, so an informal term, "Chapter Six-and-a-Half," emerged to describe such activities as conflict prevention, demobilization, cantonment of weapons, and actions taken to guarantee freedom of movement within a country. Mostly because of Cold War rivalries, only 13 U.N. peacekeeping operations were approved between 1945 and 1987. With the winding down of the Cold War, however, 13 *new ones* (not including the peace enforcement operation in Somalia) were approved between 1987 and 1992. There is another important figure that will come as no surprise to anyone who has ever stepped in to break up a barracks fight—during this same time, more than 800 peacekeepers from 43 countries have been killed while serving under the U.N. flag.

There is no doubt that the increasing number of peace operations has strained the ability of the United Nations to manage them effectively. Because it deals more with diplomacy than with control of military operations, U.N. headquarters in New York maintains a relatively small civilian staff to oversee peacekeeping operations. Another independent staff agency has traditionally handled all administrative matters, including logistics. Until recently, the organization also lacked an operations center capable of maintaining 24-hour communications with these worldwide deployments. Not every peacekeeping operation takes place under U.N. control, but those that do have no standard organization or staff structure for field operations. However, they all answer to the U.N. Secretary

General and may be headed either by his Special Representative or by a force commander whom he has selected. Because the United Nations also lacks standard doctrine, tactics, and equipment, command and control is a problem for all but small operations in generally peaceful environments.

Problems encountered with the U.N. structure during our operations in Somalia (inlcuding some of those discussed below) contributed to a Presidential Directive in May 1994 pledging U.S. support for reforms in the planning, logistics, and command and control of United Nations-sponsored peace operations. Because these reforms will take time to be agreed upon and implemented, it is especially important to note that the Directive also laid down two basic principles for the future:

• Although the President will never relinquish *command* of U.S. forces, he does have the authority to place American soldiers under the *operational control* of a foreign commander when doing so serves our national interests. The terms *command* and *operational control* are defined and discussed in chapter II. In fact, that situation has occurred on many occasions in our military history, from the Revolutionary War to *Desert Storm*.)

• The larger the peace operation, and the greater the likelihood of combat, the less likely it is that the United States will agree to surrender operational control of its forces to a U.N. commander. Participation of U.S. forces in operations likely to involve combat should be conducted under the operational control of the United States, an ad hoc coalition, or a competent regional security organization such as NATO.

Joint Doctrine

Because they are often a central focus of international attention, peace operations have a unique ability to combine the tactical, the operational, and the strategic levels of war. A single unwise tactical move by a soldier on patrol can instantly change the character of an entire operation and, when broadcast by the ever-present media pool, can also affect strategic considerations. In these and other circumstances, the joint perspective is the beginning of wisdom, with joint doctrine providing the "playbook" that allows our Armed Forces to function more effectively as a team. Although American forces began their operations in Somalia without the benefit of a standard peacekeeping doctrine, that experience suggests that the following joint doctrinal publications are especially relevant for future missions:

• The most fundamental principles by which we organize and operate are outlined in Joint Pub 0-2, *Unified Action Armed Forces* (UNAAF). This key publication provides basic doctrine and policy governing joint operations, especially command and control and the formation of joint task forces.

• Another helpful tool in joint force planning is Joint Pub 5-00.2, *Joint Task Force Planning Guidance and Procedures.* Its practical discussions and detailed checklists are designed to assist commanders and planners in translating joint policy and doctrine into operational decisions, especially on short-notice contingency operations.

• Issued during our operations in Somalia,

Joint Pub 3-0, *Doctrine for Joint Operations,* outlines the fundamental principles and concepts for joint and multinational operations and provides the basis for unit training prior to deployment. Most importantly, it specifies the following principles as guidelines for military units in operations other than war:

Objective. A clearly defined and attainable objective—with a precise understanding of what constitutes success—is critical when the United States is involved in operations other than war. Military commanders should also understand what specific conditions could result in mission termination as well as those that yield failure.

Unity of effort. The principle of unity of command in war is difficult to attain in operations other than war. In these operations, other government agencies may often have the lead, with nongovernmental organizations and humanitarian relief organizations playing important roles as well. Command arrangements may often be only loosely defined and many times will not involve command authority as we in the military customarily understand it. Commanders must seek an atmosphere of cooperation to achieve objectives by unity of effort.

Security. Nothing about peace operations changes the moral and legal responsibility of commanders at every level to take whatever actions are required to protect their forces from any threat. Inherent in this responsibility is the need to be capable of a rapid transition from normal operations to combat whenever the need arises. However, what makes this responsibility especially challenging in peace operations is the balance that must be struck with "restraint."

Restraint. Because the restoration of peace rather than a clearly defined military victory is the basic objective of these operations, military force must be applied with great caution and foresight. The restraints on weaponry, tactics, and levels of violence that characterize this environment must be clearly understood by each individual service member. Rules of engagement (ROE) are standard military procedures, but in peace operations, they will often be more restrictive, detailed, and sensitive to political concerns than in war: they may also change frequently.

Perseverance. Peace operations may require years to achieve the desired effects because the underlying causes of confrontation and conflict rarely have a clear beginning or a decisive resolution. Although this is a principle often tied to debates about U.S. long-term commitments, its operational application is that commanders must balance their desire to attain objectives quickly with a sensitivity for the long-term strategic aims that may impose some limitations on operations.

Legitimacy. Legitimacy is a function of effective control over territory, the consent of the governed, and compliance with certain international standards. Each of these factors governs the actions not only of governments but also of peacekeepers—whose presence in a country depends on the perception that there is a legitimate reason for them to be there. During operations where a government does not exist, peacekeepers must avoid actions that would effectively confer legitimacy on one individual or organization at the expense of another. Because every military move will inevitably affect the local political situation, peacekeepers must learn how to conduct operations without appearing to take sides in internal disputes between competing factions.

- Another joint doctrinal publication, Joint Pub 3-07.3, *Joint Tactics, Techniques, and Procedures for Peacekeeping Operations,* identifies certain personal qualities that need to be instilled at all levels during training for peace operations. Those individual qualities are: patience, flexibility, self-discipline, professionalism, impartiality, tact and inquisitiveness. The common factor in all these qualities is quality itself: the quality of the soldier is fundamental to everything we do—especially in the demanding environment of peace operations.

If there is a common though unstated thread running through these joint doctrinal principles, it is that diplomatic, military, and humanitarian actions must be closely integrated in any peace operation. When correctly planned and executed, each of these actions should reinforce the other: well-conceived humanitarian actions, for example, will win friends among the local populace in a way that will improve the security situation and make military tasks easier. With the benefit of hindsight, it is possible to see that operations in Somalia were successful when they recognized this trinity of diplomatic, military, and humanitarian actions— and remarkably less so when they did not.

The Effects of the Operational Environment

The difficulties of geography, transportation, and political conditions combined to pose operating challenges for American forces in Somalia.

Geography. As shown by figure 1, the country is located on a geographical feature known as the Horn of Africa on the northeastern coast of that continent. The region's remoteness from established U.S. operating facilities—24 hours by air and several weeks by sea from the United States—was further complicated by the country's size, a land mass of almost 250 million square miles, nearly the size of New England. The terrain looks much like the low desert regions of the American southwest—dry with sparse vegetation and an annual rainfall of less than 20 inches. The drought that has plagued East Africa for much of the last decade has been especially severe in Somalia, with food and water supplies scarce or, in some areas, nonexistent. Consequently, peacekeepers were forced to bring with them most, if not all, of what they would eat and drink.

Lines of Communication. The limited, 2,600-km network of paved roads runs mostly among the main coastal cities of Mogadishu, Merca, Kismayo, and Berbera; however, this network had fallen into disrepair. Interior roads are mostly unpaved, and grading and other maintenance are haphazard. Mogadishu has the country's main international airport, although there are seven other paved airstrips throughout the country. Cleared airstrips in the back country are the only other

FIGURE 1. *Somalia*

U.S. and Somalia
Relative Size

complement to the limited air transportation network. Somalia has a long coastline, but harbor facilties are either undeveloped or have fallen into disrepair. Mogadishu, Kismayo, and Berbera have only limited cargo handling facilities. Because widespread civil unrest made normal maintenance and repair impossible, there was no functioning telephone system in Somalia. The combined effects of these factors made mobility and communications consistent problems for peace operations— especially when measured against the need to help feed thousands of starving people.

The freighter PVT FRANKLIN J. PHILLIPS pulls into Kismayo, delivering supplies and food stuffs in support of Operation Restore Hope.

Political. Although drought conditions were partially responsible for this situation, civil war had devastated this already threatened country. Since 1988, this civil war has centered around more than 14 clans and factions that make up Somali society, all of which fought for control of their own territory. Their culture stresses the idea of "me and my clan against all outsiders," with alliances between clans being only temporary conveniences. Guns and aggressiveness, including the willingness to accept casualties, are intrinsic parts of this culture, with women and children considered part of the clan's order of battle. Because the area was for more than a decade a focal point for Cold War rivalries, large amounts of individual and heavy weapons found their way from government control to clan armories. After the fall of the Siad Barre regime in 1991, the political situation deteriorated, with the clans in the northern part of the country trying to secede. With drought conditions worsening everywhere, clan warfare and banditry gradually spread throughout Somalia. By early 1992, these conditions brought about a famine of Biblical proportions: more than *one-half million* Somalis had perished of starvation and at least a million more were threatened. Somalia had become a geographical expression rather than a country—but whatever it was called, the scale of the human suffering there had now captured the attention of the international community.

Situations and Missions

U.S. involvement in Somalia proceeded through three stages: Operation *Provide Relief*, a humanitarian assistance mission; Operation

Restore Hope, an operation that combined humanitarian assistance with limited military action; and UNOSOM II, a peace enforcement mission involving active combat and nation-building (figure 2). From the beginning of the effort to relieve the suffering in Somalia, however, there were two basic problems: moving enough food, water, and medicine into the country, and providing security to protect the relief supplies from theft by bandits or confiscation by the clans and warring factions. In April 1992, the U.N. Security Council approved Resolution 751, establishing the United Nations Operation in Somalia—UNOSOM—whose mission was to provide humanitarian aid and facilitate the end of hostilities in Somalia. The 50 UNOSOM observers sent in did not make a noticeable difference in either ending hostilities or securing relief supplies but in July, the United Nations asked for increased airlifts for food. President Bush responded by ordering U.S. forces to support Operation *Provide Relief* from 15 August 1992 through 9 December 1992.

Organized by CENTCOM, the mission of this operation was to "provide military assistance in support of emergency humanitarian relief to Kenya and Somalia." Among its objectives:

• Deploy a Humanitarian Assistance Survey Team (HAST) to assess relief requirements in Kenya and Somalia

• Activate a Joint Task Force to conduct an emergency airlift of food and supplies into Somalia and Northern Kenya

• Deploy (4) C-141 aircraft and (8) C-130 aircraft to Mombasa and Wajir, Kenya to provide daily relief sorties into Somalia during daylight hours to locations which provide a permissive and safe environment.

During the 6 months of Operation *Provide Relief,* a daily average of 20 sorties delivered approximately 150 metric tons of supplies; in total, more than 28,000 metric tons of critically needed relief supplies were brought into Somalia by this airlift.

FIGURE 2: *Three phases of U.S. involvement in Somalia*

Operation	Dates	UN Security Council Resolution	U.S. Commander
Provide Relief (UNOSOM I)	15 Aug 1992- 9 Dec 1992	UNSCR# 751 dtd 24 Apr 1992	(HAST-then JTF) BG Frank Libutti, USMC
Restore Hope (UNITAF)	9 Dec 1992- 4 May 1993	UNSCR# 794 dtd 3 Dec 1992	LTG Robert B. Johnston, USMC
USFORSOM (UNOSOM II)	4 May 1993- 31 Mar 1994	UNSCR# 814 dtd 26 Mar 1993	MG Thomas M. Montgomery, USA

Despite the reinforcement of UNOSOM throughout the next several months, the security situation grew worse. In November, a ship laden with relief supplies was fired upon in the harbor at

Mogadishu, forcing its withdrawal before the badly needed supplies could be brought ashore. In the United States and elsewhere, public distress grew and, on 4 December 1992, President George Bush announced the initiation of Operation *Restore Hope*. Under the terms of U.N. Resolution 794 (passed the previous day), the United States would both lead and provide military forces to a multinational coalition to be known as the United Task Force, or UNITAF. This force would bridge the gap until the sitation stabilized enough for it to be turned over to a permanent U.N. peacekeeping force. The U.N. mandate implied two important missions: to provide humanitarian assistance to the Somali people, and to restore order in southern Somalia. Because of the implicit requirement to use force in establishing a secure environment for the distribution of relief supplies, it is significant that the mandate referred to Chapter VII of the U.N. Charter.

The CENTCOM mission statement clearly reflected these objectives: "When directed by the NCA, USCINCCENT will conduct joint/combined military operations in Somalia to secure the major air and sea ports, key installations and food distribution points, to provide open and free passage of relief supplies, provide security for convoys and relief organization operations, and assist UN/NGO's in providing humanitarian relief under U.N. auspices. Upon establishing a secure environment for uninterrupted relief operations, USCINCCENT terminates and transfers relief operations to U.N. peacekeeping forces."

U.S. Navy Seabees from Naval Mobile Construction Battalion 1 pour concrete floors in classrooms as part of a civic action program of Operation Restore Hope.

During its existence from 9 December 1992 through 4 May 1993, UNITAF ultimately involved more than 38,000 troops from 21 coalition nations, including 28,000 Americans. It clearly succeeded in its missions of stabilizing the security situation—especially by confiscating "technicals," the crew-served weapons mounted on trucks and other wheeled vehicles. With better security, more relief supplies were distributed throughout the country, staving off the immediate threat of starvation in many areas. However, plans for the termination of UNITAF and an orderly handoff of its functions to the permanent peacekeeping force, christened UNOSOM II, were repeatedly put off.   U.N. Secretary-General Boutros-Ghali urged delay until

U.S. forces could effectively disarm the bandits and rival clan factions that continued to operate throughout Somalia. In addition, he proposed to rebuild the country's fragmented institutions "from the top down"—an exercise akin to nation-building.

These disagreements delayed but did not ultimately prevent the formation of UNOSOM II, officially established by Security Council Resolution 814 on 26 March 1993. The Resolution was significant in several ways:

• The Council mandated the first ever U.N.-directed peacekeeping operation under the Chapter VII enforcement provisions of the Charter, including the requirement for UNOSOM II to disarm the Somali clans

• It explicitly endorsed the objective of rehabilitating the political institutions and economy of a member state

• It called for building a secure environment throughout the country, including the northern region that had declared its independence.

These far-reaching objectives went well beyond the much more limited mandate of UNITAF as well as those of any previous U.N. operation. To implement them, a full U.N. peacekeeping structure was set up in Somalia, headed by retired U.S. Navy Admiral Jonathan Howe as Special Representative of the Secretary General with Turkish Lieutenant General Cevik Bir as force commander of the U.N. multinational contingent.

Rather than being in charge, U.S. participation in this operation was primarily conceived in terms of logistical support, with over 3,000 personnel specifically committed to that mission. Significantly, however, the United States was also asked to provide a Quick Reaction Force—some 1,150 soldiers from the US Army's 10th Mountain Division—that would operate under the tactical control of the Commander, U.S. Forces, Somalia. The mission of the 4,500 American forces supporting UNOSOM II from 4 May 1993 to 31 March 1994 was as follows: "When directed, UNOSOM II Force Command conducts military operations to consolidate, expand, and maintain a secure environment for the advancement of humanitarian aid, economic assistance, and political reconciliation in Somalia."

Major General Thomas Montgomery receives back briefs with the U.S. Quick Reaction Force.

The ambitious U.N. mandate as well as the continuing presence of the multinational contingent ultimately threatened the Mogadishu power base of one clan warlord, Mohammed Aideed. The crisis came into full view on 5 June 1993, when 24 Pakistani soldiers were killed in an ambush by Aideed supporters. The United Nations Security Council Resolution 837, passed the next day, called for the immediate apprehension of those responsible—and quickly led to U.S. forces being used in a highly personalized manhunt for Aideed. After a series of clashes involving U.S. Rangers and other units, a major engagement occurred on 3 October in which 18 Americans were killed and 75 wounded—the bloodiest battle of any U.N. peacekeeping operation. Shortly thereafter, President Clinton announced the phased withdrawal of American troops that would end by 31 March 1994. U.S. forces largely were confined to force protection missions from this change of mission until the withdrawal was completed.

II. OPERATIONAL LESSONS LEARNED

None of the political leadership can tell me what they want me to accomplish. That fact, however, does not stop them from continually asking me when I will be done.

An Anonymous U.N. Commander en route
to a Peace Operation

Each of the three distinctly different phases of our operations in Somalia—*Provide Relief, Restore Hope*, and UNOSOM II—can teach future U.S. peacekeepers some important lessons about four areas covered in this chaper: the planning, deployment, conduct and support of peacekeeping operations.

Planning

The job of the mission planner is always thankless: anticipating requirements even before a mission statement has been formalized, orchestrating literally thousands of details that cause an operation to be successful or to go at all, adjusting those details when the concept of the operation changes, and doing all of these things under time pressures that would cause breakdowns in lesser mortals. The CENTCOM planners involved in all phases of the Somalia operations lived up to this job description, in addition to adapting formerly standard procedures to new and uncertain tasks. Perhaps they recalled the words attributed to General Eisenhower, himself a former war planner: "Plans are useless, but planning is essential."

Mandates and Missions

Lessons

• **Clear U.N. mandates are critical to the planning of the mission because they shape the basic political guidance given to U.S. forces by our National Command Authorities (NCA). A clear mandate shapes not only the mission (the *what*) that we perform but the way we carry it out (the *how*).**

• **Second only to the basic structure of command, the organization of the Joint Task Force (JTF) is key because it must balance the needs of continuity with the integration of additional capabilities. Organizational methods include augmenting an existing headquarters or earmarking a standard but adaptible contingency package: but the selection of the nucleus should be driven by standard mission essential factors, such as mission, enemy, troops, terrain, and time available.**

Examples

Prior to establishing the airlift for *Provide Relief,* CENTCOM dispatched a Humanitarian Assistance Survey Team to Somalia. No sooner had they arrived than the team found they had been reconstituted as the nucleus for the operation's JTF. Despite the fact that both the mandate and the mission seemed clear, the JTF soon found itself coordinating a 6-month operation that eventually delivered 28,000 metric tons of supplies. Their mission also came to include airlifting Pakistani peacekeepers into the country as well as conducting delicate negotiations with clan warlords to assure the security of relief supplies.

The much larger scope of *Restore Hope* was reflected in the designation of a Marine Expeditionary Force headquarters as the nucleus for the JTF. Although this choice inescapably lent a "Marine Corps flavor" to the operation, it also lent a continuity of relationships and procedures that was critical in view of the larger problems faced by the JTF. Its particular challenge was to head a multinational coalition of 20 different countries—many of them chosen more to demonstrate broad international support for the U.N. mandate than to provide complementary military capabilities. Even more daunting was the need to align these operations with the activities of as many as 49 different U.N. and humanitarian relief agencies—none of which was obligated to follow military directives.

Not only was unity of command a challenge in these circumstances but there was a span of control problem that offers an object lesson for future planners, because the size of the military units forming the multinational contingent varied from platoon to brigade. A reasonable span of control was worked out, with the major participants contributing brigade-size units that could be given mission-type orders (figure 3). Several smaller contingents were placed under the Army and Air Force components, while nine countries were placed under Marine control, as they had responsibility for securing the Mogadishu area. (However, national sensitivities do not always allow such integration into a standard military hierarchy because subordination could imply a slight to national sovereignty—and certain national governments have expressly prohibited this type of relationship.)

Two other important span of control innovations under UNITAF included a Civil-Military Operations Center and the division of the country into nine Humanitarian Relief Sectors that allowed both the distribution of food and the assignment of military areas of responsibility. The relatively crisp mandate was also important in avoiding subsequent urgings by U.N. officials for UNITAF to become more deeply engaged in disarming the clans; instead, the commander limited the confiscations to those individual weapons, "technicals," and arms caches that were a clear threat to his force.

The U.S. mission to support UNOSOM II, by contrast, was considerably more open-ended, although this fact may not have been well appreciated when the operation began. The basic command arrangements reflected the fact that the operation was to take place under U.N. control, with U.S. Major General Thomas M. Montgomery acting both as Commander, U.S. Forces Somalia (USFORSOM), and as deputy to the U.N. Force Commander in Somalia, Lieutenant General Cevik Bir. The potential for conflict in this dual-hatting of command relationships was clear: as a U.S. Commander, MG Montgomery served under the command and control of CENTCOM, while as deputy to General Bir, he served under the operational control of the United Nations. Even more significant, however, was the fact that General Montgomery carried out his responsibilities through an unusual arrangement of operational and tactical control over assigned U.S. forces. These key distinctions in levels of authority are shown in figure 4; their implications are discussed in pages 53-74.

Commander, Central Command, General Hoar is greeted by LtGen Johnston, commander of Restore Hope *at Mogadishu Airport.*

Although General Montgomery was given only 4,500 troops—many of them logistical personnel— his combat missions included force protection, manning an organic quick reaction force, providing for use of off-shore augmentation to the quick reaction force, and armed aerial reconnaisance. Complicating these responsibilities was the fact that MG Montgomery met the UNOSOM II staff for the first time when he arrived in Somalia—and only 30 percent of them had arrived by the time the mission was launched. Unlike the UNITAF staff, the USFORSOM headquarters was not built around a well-formed central nucleus but was brought together in some haste—composed primarily of Army officers individually recruited from the Army Staff and units worldwide.

While there may have been some expectations that such staff arrangements were all that was needed in a situation in which the United States no longer had the lead, foot-dragging by U.N. officials further complicated the transition between UNITAF and UNOSOM II. The initial slowness in setting up the UNOSOM II staff was aggravated by its composition; it was formed incrementally from the voluntary contributions of the multinational contingents who detailed personnel as they arrived. There certainly was an urgent need under these circumstances to insure a proper handoff between the key staffs of the incoming and outgoing U.S. components. General Johnston has pointed out that there was approximately a 6-week overlap between the UNITAF and UNOSOM II staffs, that the incoming and outgoing staff counterparts were co-located, and that detailed SOPs were jointly

FIGURE 3. *UNITAF Somalia (top) and UNISOM II and USFORSOM*

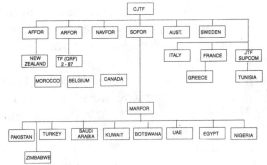

UNITAF SOMALIA
PHASE III & PHASE IV COMMAND RELATIONSHIPS

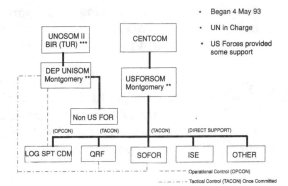

UNISOM II AND USFORSOM

- Began 4 May 93
- UN in Charge
- US Forces provided some support

prepared to aid in the transition. These were clearly important steps, but it also can be argued that the real issues were the lack of agreement between the United States and the United Nations about the conditions at the time of the transition and the military capabilities required to carry out the expanded mandate of UNOSOM II. Those issues go well beyond the scope of operational command, but it is clear from subsequent events that the underlying causes of conflict in Somalia had only been postponed. Those conflicts exploded into the open and largely defined the development of the UNOSOM II mission—a fact that can only suggest for the future that, if such transitions cannot be avoided altogether, they should at least be jointly developed by the incoming and the outgoing force.

Mission Analysis: Entry and Exit Strategies

Lessons

• Although they are to some extent implied by the mission, entry and exit strategies are important planning criteria: they govern how we should expect to go in and under what conditions we can expect to get out.

• One major military responsibility in a peace operation is determining and measuring success—keeping the chain of command informed as to where we are between entry and exit while avoiding the inevitable pressures of "mission creep."

Examples

Because it was relatively brief, the *Provide Relief*

FIGURE 4: *Levels of authority*

TERM	DEFINITION
Combatant Command (COCOM)	•Nontransferable command authority established by law. •Provides full authority to organize and employ commands and forces as the combatant commander considers necessary to accomplish assigned missions.
Operational Control (OPCON)	•Transferable command authority that may be exercised by commanders at any echelon at or below the level of combatant command. •Includes authoritative direction over all aspects of military operations and joint training necessary to accomplish missions assigned to the command. •Does not include authoritative direction for logistics or matters of administration, discipline, internal organization, or unit training.
Tactical Control (TACON)	•Command authority over assigned or attached forces or commands or military capability made available for tasking. •Limited to the detailed and usually local direction and control of movements or maneuvers necessary to accomplish assigned missions or tasks. Source: Joint Pub. 1-02

airlift provided few tough entry or exit questions, beyond the obvious ones of security for the in-country ground crews. The criterion for success was similarly clear: provide food supplies to get people past the immediate threat of starvation. The entry of UNITAF was semipermissive, the only real "opposition" for a time coming from television camera crews on the landing beaches. The well-understood U.N. mandate helped keep the focus on the most important criteria for success: better security and more food distribution. The exit strategy was implicit in the handoff to UNOSOM II, an event that identified both a specific time frame and milestones such as the building of a staff. When these milestones were not reached, it clearly flagged a problem: how that problem was handled, however, is another matter. Although the handoff was not complete, U.S. forces were withdrawn on schedule. While their departure certainly represented a successful conclusion of the UNITAF mission (as well as a useful signal to U.N. officials), the lack of an effective transition clearly complicated conditions for both the entry and the exit for U.S. forces supporting UNOSOM II.

Although both UNITAF and UNOSOM were authorized as peace-enforcement missions under Chapter VII of the U.N. Charter, the UNOSOM II mandate reflected a considerably deeper commitment of both security and humanitarian assistance. This mandate, however, was not by itself an invitation to the increasing use of U.S. forces in combat situations. In fact, those who originally committed the United States to a role in UNOSOM II believed that American forces would primarily play a role in logistical support to the operation. The 1,150 American troops constituting the Quick Reaction Force (QRF) were to provide a rapid response only when specific threats, attacks, or other emergencies exceeded the capabilities of other UNOSOM II forces. They were expressly barred from spearheading routine operations, escorting convoys, or providing other longer term security actions. However, there was an inadequate appreciation by planners for a potential adversary who turned out to be highly resourceful and capable of adapting to the forces brought against him. In the aftermath of the 5 June ambush that killed 24 Pakistani peacekeepers, the United States played a prominent role in drafting U.N. Security Concil Resolution 837, which called for the apprehension of those parties responsible. That resolution constituted another de facto change in the mission, because its terms were rapidly translated into a manhunt for Mohammed Aideed. Because those operations clearly outran the capabilities of other UNOSOM II forces, there was an immediate expansion in the use of the Quick Reation Force—now backed up by armed helicopters from the 10th Mountain Division as well as Air Force AC-130 gunships. Ultimately, the manhunt for Aideed led to the commitment of Task Force Ranger and to the climactic battle in Mogadishu on the night of 3-4 October 1993.

This deepening involvement of U.S. forces in combat operations during UNOSOM II has been criticized as "mission creep," despite the fact that these changes in both mission and direction clearly resulted from specific decisions reached by the national command authorities. However, the important lesson for future planners that can be derived from this experience is that the best way to avoid mission creep is to analyze what the mission really calls for; this means constantly measuring the mission against milestones that best indicate its success or failure. The choice of milestones is especially important. In peace operations, these measures should not normally be expressed in terms of enemy killed and wounded or kilometers of ground taken; if they are, this is itself an indicator that the peace operation has changed in ways that should call into question both the mission and the mandate. In fact, the best measures of success may well be those that signal reductions in the level of violence. Other important indicators may be expressed in terms of the numbers of children being fed, gallons of potable water being pumped, or weapons being turned in. While specific criteria will depend upon the mission, all must be capable of answering one basic question: "How will we know when we have won?"

Multinational Contingents
Lessons

• Because multinational forces are ad hoc coalitions of the willing, planners must recognize the reduced tempo with which a coalition force conducts peace operations.

• Different national capabilities and international differences also affect both the planning and the reality of peace operations.

Examples

Even though it was not part of a formal coalition, the emergency airlift of *Provide Relief* brought its participants into immediate contact with other nations providing relief aid, as well as the added responsibility of transporting Pakistani peacekeepers into Somalia. This lesson illustrates that, like most neighborhood and community associations, all coalitions are voluntary, bringing with them a mixture of strengths and limitations, friendships and rivalries. As Joint Pub 3-07.3 notes, terms of reference must pin down the most critical elements relating to a country's participation in a peace operation: command relationships, organization, logistical responsibilities, and even accounting procedures. The difference was that in *Restore Hope* these terms of reference were primarily negotiated through the United States as the leader of the coalition, while with UNOSOM II, these terms were negotiated with the United Nations.

No serious problems appear to have arisen among the multinational contingents supporting *Restore Hope*, possibly as the result of a sensible decision to have the major contributing countries send liaison officers to CENTCOM for coordination prior to dispatching their forces to Somalia. General Johnston has also noted that the command arrangements outlined above achieved both unity of command and unity of purpose, despite the challenges of leading a large and diverse coalition:

> Our coalition partners had signed up to the rules of engagement and the basic humanitarian mission and in every instance sought to have a close bilateral arrangement with the U.S. Commander. They . . . reported to me daily on activities with periodic formal and comprehensive briefings on progress. *Unity of command can be achieved when everyone signs up to the mission and to the command relationship.* (emphasis added)

However, with the increasing intensity of combat during UNOSOM II, adherence to the U.N. terms of reference became more problematical. Because most multinational contingents—including ours—make it a point to stay in close touch with their national capitals, concerns over the policy of hunting for Aideed grew along with the increased potential for combat. The challenge of commanding a coalition force under these circumstances can be seen in the subsequent statement of UNOSOM II Commander Lieutenant General Bir, who cited his lack of command authority over the assigned forces as the most significant limitation of this operation or any other one organized under Chapter VII. Certainly the authority of future U.N. force commanders is a topic that will be hotly debated for some time to come.

Another critical element for the planner is the difference between what is planned for and what shows up. It is a basic fact of international life that many of the poorer countries that have regularly participated in peace operations have done so because duty with the United Nations pays a portion of their military budgets. Equipment considered standard—even basic—in most western armies is simply not present in the inventories of many military contingents from developing countries. This fact was evident during UNOSOM II when some of the contingents that had volunteered for a Chapter VI (peacekeeping) mission arrived lacking the minimal gear required for Chapter VII (peace enforcement) operations. The U.N. commander thus had the dual challenges of providing these contingents with the equipment they needed (often from U.S. stocks) as well as the logistical support needed to keep that equipment operating. The equipment multinationals do bring with them is not likely to be interoperable, so that identifying the most critical items that must be made to work together is especially important—communications and ammunition calibers being two of the more obvious examples.

Rules of Engagement (ROE)

Lessons

- **ROE are not only life and death decisions but also critical elements in determining the success or failure of a peace operation: that means that the determination of ROE is a command decision.**

- **As important as they are, ROE are effective only to the extent that they can be understood and applied by the forces carrying out a peace operation: that means keeping the ROE simple, direct, and unclassified.**

Examples

ROE, common in any military operation, are especially important in a peace operation because they provide the means for applying (or not applying) deadly force in a situation in which the objective is normally to avoid or to minimize violence. ROE embody two of the most important principles from operations other than war—restraint and legitimacy—because the use of force must be seen as supporting the ends for which the operation was begun in the first place. The ROE in effect for *Restore Hope* and UNOSOM II involved three issues: the proper use of force, the confiscation and disposition of weapons, and the handling of civilians detained by military forces. The most critical issue involved the use of force and the circumstances in which it was authorized.

With admirable simplicity, the UNITAF ROE listed four basic "no's:"

- No "technicals," such as trucks carrying mounted machine guns
- No banditry
- No roadblocks
- No visible weapons.

Because crew-served weapons—such as the technicals—were seen as particular threats regardless of whether the crew demonstrated hostile intent, UNITAF commanders were authorized to use "all necessary force" to confiscate and demilitarize them. But what did "all necessary force" really mean? Did it amount to "shoot on sight?" UNITAF commander Marine Lieutenant General Robert Johnston decided it did not and directed commanders to challenge and approach the technicals, using all necessary force if the weapons were not voluntarily surrendered. Similar approaches were used in confiscating arms caches. These rules, combined with the demonstration of overwhelming force by UNITAF, resulted in few challenges to forcible confiscation efforts—and surprisingly few acts of violence directed against U.S. forces.

When the 20,000 U.S. soldiers of UNITAF were replaced by the 4,500 supporting UNOSOM II, these ROE were initially left unchanged. With the changes in mission and forces, however, violence escalated and resulted in Fragmentary Order 39, issued by the U.N. force commander, which stated: "Organized, armed militias, technicals, and other crew served weapons are considered a threat to UNOSOM Forces *and may be engaged without provocation*" (emphasis added). There is a direct line of continuity between that rule and the increasing involvement of U.S. forces in combat operations. There was a noticeable difference as well in the way U.S. forces interpreted the ROE, stressing aggressive enforcement, while other national contingents emphasized more graduated responses before using deadly force. Frag. Order 39 continued in effect until after U.S. forces were in a force protection posture pending their withdrawal. In January 1994, after a Marine sniper team engaged a machine gunner atop a bus, the ROE were again amended to exclude targets where collateral damage could not be controlled.

These experiences suggest that ROE should be applied as the direct result of carefully considered command decisions, decisions that calibrate the nature of the threat with the balance that must be struck between the often competing requirements of restraint and the security of the force. It should be clear that the Rules of Engagement must be written not only with the "KISS" principle (Keep It Simple, Stupid) in mind but also with an appreciation for how they might be applied in tense situations by warfighters rather than lawyers. Classified ROE not only detract from those objectives but also make little sense in a multinational coalition with the native population closely observing and taking advantage of every move. In fact, there is an advantage to ensuring that ROE are provided to the belligerents, who need to know and firmly understand the rules of the game. Finally, while on-scene commanders must generally be free to modify ROE to reflect conditions on the ground, frequent changes in the ROE should be avoided. The old military maxim, "Order—Counter-order—Disorder" applies to these vital rules as well. Keep the ROE simple and try to keep them consistent.

Personnel Selection and Training

Lesson

The selection and training of personnel are just as important for peace operations as for more conventional military operations—and maybe even more so.

Examples

All three phases of the Somalia operation underline the importance of this lesson as well as the more fundamental point that the quality of the soldier is basic to everything we do as a military force. Just as in other operations, success depends directly on the patient investments in training time and effort made during the months and years before the actual deployment order is received. Anticipation of such missions helps as well, with unit commanders who are able to build on those capabilities and hone the individual skills of their troops to a fine edge. Success in peacekeeping operations depends directly upon small-unit tactical competence and the bedrock mastery of basic military skills.

Some understanding of the differences between Chapter VI peacekeeping requirements and Chapter VII enforcement action is needed as well. In peacekeeping, Joint Pub 3-07.3 effectively sums up the required mindset:

> Peacekeeping requires an adjustment of attitude and approach by the individual to a set of circumstances different from those normally found on the field of battle—an adjustment to suit the needs of peaceable intervention rather than of an enforcement action.

In addition to the individual character traits discussed by that publication, the most important ones are probably good judgment and independent action.

Enforcement actions require all these things in addition to the ability to transition rapidly to full-scale combat operations when required. MG Montgomery has noted the need for more effective predeployment training standards, including the in-theater ROEs, local culture, and weapons familiarization. One reason for suggesting these improvements was provided by the Army's 43rd Engineer Battalion, a heavy construction unit that participated in UNOSOM II. The unit was given very short notice prior to its deployment, but to make matters worse it was one of the many Army units beginning the process of de-activation. Not only were its complements of personnel and equipment less than expected for deployment, but herculean efforts were required by the soldiers of this battalion (as well as other units) to accomplish the mission.

One final point: peace operations put a premium on certain specialists who should be identified early and placed near the front of any deployment—possibly on the first plane. They include: trained Joint Operations Planning and Execution System (JOPES) operators, contract specialists (especially those with experience in local procurement), logisticians, lawyers, medical specialists, WWMCCS operators, port transportation organizers, public affairs officers, military police, combat engineers, psychological operations specialists (PSYOPS), and civil affairs experts, as well as special forces teams. Equally important are people with specific knowledge of the language and the country. Because there was a shortage of people with a working knowledge of the Somali language, linguists were recruited by contract both in the United States and Somalia. Although this recruitment raised some obvious questions of operations security, the program proved very effective for most situations. The use of

Reserve Component personnel with special qualifications for service in Somalia also worked well—suggesting the importance of Reserve Component integration in the planning of future peace operations.

Joint Planning

Lessons

• **Planning for peace operations is much the same as planning for combat operations—except that peace operations are typically smaller and involve more fine tuning.**

• **Turbulence is a constant: it is what happens when you have to balance the management requirements to plan an operation with the flexibility needed by those who will soon be carrying it out.**

• **While it may have certain flaws, the Joint Operations Planning and Execution System (JOPES) is the baseline system for all U.S. deployments, including those supporting peace operations.**

Examples

The 28,000 troops deployed during *Restore Hope* clearly presented the most challenging planning problems, beginning with the longer lead times now needed to establish "strategic air bridges" with U.S. bases and other facilities being reduced worldwide. Given the air distances between the United States and Somalia, overflight rights, refuelling and en-route support arrangements required additional time and effort to arrange. Current information on the capacities and conditions of both air and marine terminals in Somalia was also lacking. Under those conditions, it seemed particularly unfortunate that CENTCOM delayed until late in the deployment the arrival of so-called "transportation through-putters." Because these soldiers are trained to unscramble delays at such terminals, it would make better sense in future deployments to have them in country sooner rather than later.

One of the most perceptive reports to emerge from *Restore Hope* noted that the initial stages of a deployment always place great demands upon a very limited infrastructure, but especially in a case like Somalia. That situation was compounded because, in the words of the report,

> In contingencies, the tendency is for everyone to consider themselves to be of such great importance that their presence is required in-country first. Not everyone can or should be first. . . . Higher rank should not translate into higher precedence for arriving in-country.

A better approach for the future, it suggested, may be to organize JTF headquarters in modules, each with its associated logistics and communications, and to deploy them in successive stages as capabilities are added to the force. This seems to be a reasonable approach when dealing with a particularly austere operational environment while allowing JTF commanders a better opportunity to tailor forces and their support to the specific situation at hand.

Some of the more consistent criticisms concern the way that joint planning influenced the way UNOSOM II was "stood up." Much of this process appears to have been surprisingly random, perhaps because this was the first time that American forces had been committed to a U.N.-led peace enforcement operation. However, the ultimate result was that in Somalia MG Montgomery confronted a situation in which his command was constructed not as a result of a joint blueprint carefully modified to reflect his circumstances, but rather as the result of a considerably more convoluted planning process. One example: the J6 (communications) staff was not assigned to the JTF early enough to influence communications plannning, and the J6 director himself did not arrive in country until 2 weeks after the activation of UNOSOM II.

Consistently strong opinions were expressed about the JOPES during all phases of the Somalia operation. Complaints included the system's lack of user-friendliness, the inflexibility of its procedures, and the difficulty of importing data from other sources. Most observers, however, correctly note that the system is a powerful planning tool that is also the backbone of the joint operations system. The system's advocates echo the point that JOPES takes discipline and practice, ideally with specifically trained personnel. Clearly, you don't want to go to either war or peace operations without JOPES-smart operators. Even when they are present, however, it is best to remember that there is a built-in conflict between the discipline needed to run that system and the flexibility demanded by those that JOPES and similar planning systems are supposed to support.

A good example of what can go wrong with the best of intentions was provided by ARCENT (Army Forces, Central Command) planners just prior to *Restore Hope*. Those planners put great time and thought into the construction of the Time-Phased Force Deployment Document (TPFDD) and loaded it into the JOPES data base for implementation by subordinate commands. Unfortunately, these subordinate commands had been given "write permission" on the TPFDD and began to make changes with a vengeance. Within hours, wholesale changes to unit types, personnel, equipment, and deployment dates had been entered—largely making a hash of ARCENT's careful arrangements. JOPES operators at ARCENT—now presumably armed— labored for weeks to make the hundreds of corrections required to ensure that people, equipment, and lift were in proper alignment. Thereafter, the authority to make changes was retained by the higher command.

Deployment

Possibly because they have a job almost as thankless as the joint planner, those who actually conduct deployments of operational forces like to remind us that amateurs talk about strategy, while professionals talk about logistics. Both topics come together in the execution of the basic elements of power projection: airlift, sealift, and pre-positioned equipment. The major share of the responsibility for deployment rests with TRANSCOM, but, as they are also quick to point out, much of their success depends upon other people. There should be no doubt, however, about the success of this deployment to Somalia. During *Restore Hope,* for example, 986 airlift missions (including both military and commercial aircraft) moved over 33,000 passengers and more than 32,000 short tons of cargo to Somalia. Eleven ships—including five fast-sealift vessels—moved 365,000 "measurement" tons of cargo to the theater as well as 1,192 containers of sustainment supplies. And over 14 million gallons of fuel were delivered from Ready Reserve Force tankers to the forces ashore.

Airlift

Lessons

• **Although airlift usually accounts for about 5 percent of a total deployment, it is a very critical 5 percent—especially in peace operations.**

• **Data have to be managed as much as any other aspect of the operation—because small bookkeeping errors can cause very large problems.**

Examples

Airlift is critical to a peace operation for two reasons: in most cases it is the fastest way to respond to a crisis and, until the arrival of sealift, it is the only way to sustain the initial deployments of peacekeepers. These were especially important considerations throughout the Somalia operations because the Mogadishu airport was capable of handling no more than two aircraft at a time. These space limitations were a special problem during *Provide Relief*, when there was no centralized airlift control, either for those aircraft chartered by international relief organizations or operated by the U.S. Government. One important innovation during this phase of the operation was the use of the Airborne Command, Control, and Communications System (ABCCC). The use of ABCCC aircraft in a primitive operating environment provided a range of critical capabilities—especially communications relay and airlift coordination—that may well suggest a model for future operations in similar areas.

Despite the remarkable success of the airlift, forecasting was a problem in two areas: the shipment of hazardous cargo (usually weapons and ammunition) and the movement of sustainment supplies (food, water and other consumables). Hazardous cargo always requires diplomatic clearances and becomes an especially sensitive issue when commercial carriers are being chartered. The movement of sustainment supplies became a problem early in *Provide Hope* because of the lack of an interface between JOPES and the Military Standard Transportation & Movement Procedures (MILSTAMP) documentation—difficulties surmounted only through extensive work-arounds.

Data differences also caused problems with the Time-Phased Force Deployment Document supporting both *Restore Hope* and UNOSOM II. Because the TPFDD expresses the CINC's decision concerning the kinds of units sent on an operation as well as the time they will enter the deployment, it is built around Unit Line Numbers (ULN) that reflect a unit's position in the deployment operations order. Army units, however, organize most of their deployment data by Unit Identity Codes (UIC) and Unit Type Codes (UTC). Because these codes do not match, there was great difficulty in manipulating the data and insuring that scarce airlift assets were not wasted.

The inevitable inaccuracies in TPFDD information also caused a recurrence of the persistent problem of in-transit visibility—the "where-is-it-now?" transportation predicament that afflicts the movement of household goods as well as the deployment of armies. In some instances, for example, telephone calls, faxes, and repeated visual checks were needed to verify that the airfield "ramp reality" matched the airlift requirements listed in the automated data base. Finally, the requests for airlift support from coalition forces during UNOSOM II routinely set unrealistic delivery dates that were themselves based more on administrative guesswork than well-constructed requirements.

Sealift

Lessons

• As with airlift, data have to be managed as much as any other aspect of the operation—because small bookkeeping errors can cause very large problems.

• The "other 95 percent" of a deployment's total requirements that come by sea offer the best opportunity to build a base which will sustain peace operations for as long as the mission requires. However, the joint perspective here is just

as important as in other areas of deployment planning.

Examples

The data management problem experienced with airlift was also encountered in sealift. Hazardous cargo was not always forecasted, for example, and inaccurate entry information as well as differences between UICs and ULN's led to problems of in-transit visibility. A new data system called EASI-LINK was instituted to help correct the visibility problem; while it showed promise, it was not completely successful in overcoming the different data formats. The net effect of the continuing difficulty in managing TPFDD information—including late changes, inaccurate entries, and unreliable information—made sealift planning as consistent a problem as it had been for airlift.

Several coordination issues underlined the fact that in logistics the integration of joint and service perspectives is not always clear. One of the most basic problems was over command and control of the seaport of Mogadishu—a critical concern because the port facilities were in such disrepair that *only one ship* could be handled at a time. There was some confusion over whether the Navy, Marine Corps, or Army was to be in charge of this "common user seaport" because the Army transportation unit doctrinally charged with the mission did not arrive until well after the first pre-positioned ships were waiting outside the port (a point discussed in the next section). The Marines on at least one occasion held back some shipping in order to supply their own requirements, despite the fact that all sealift resources were supposed to be centrally managed. And while components from within a service routinely transferred equipment from rotating to arriving units, the same arrangement did not always hold true among the services. For example, the Army at one point in the operation requested lift to ship Humvees back to its home stations—just as the Marines were requesting equally daunting lift requirements to ship their Humvees from the United States to Somalia.

Pre-positioned Shipping

Lesson

• **When other lift assets are strained by both the physical limits of geography and the time-sensitive requirements for crisis action, it is imperative that pre-positioned shipping be available to the deploying forces when they need it most. In at least one instance during the Somalia operation, Army pre-positioned shipping was unable to meet this fundamental requirement.**

Examples

There is no question that pre-positioned shipping was a valuable asset in Somalia. In particular, Marine Corps Maritime Prepositioned Ships (MPS) were able to offload essential equipment and supplies early in the deployment, despite the austerity of the port facilities. The ready availability of this logistical support not only reduced airlift burdens but also allowed UNITAF to adapt the MPS equipment packages to the unique requirements of a peacekeeping operation.   However, a useful lesson was also demonstrated by the problems experienced with three pre-positioned ships that carried equipment for all the services. During the initial phases of *Restore Hope*, these ships were unable to offload their cargo because of a combination of rough seas and inadequate port facilities. Although intelligence information on Mogadishu was somewhat lacking, it was known that the drafts of all three vessels made it impossible for them actually to enter the harbor at Mogadishu; fortunately, however, all three had the capacity to offload "in the stream." But rough seas and the delay in deploying the Army transportation specialists required to unload the vessels forced a change in plans. One of the ships moved to Kismayo, but found conditions there little better. Another went on to Mombasa, but since sealift officials had not contacted Kenyan authorities to clear unloading of the hazardous cargo (ammunition) carried by the ship, it was denied entry to the port and returned to Mogadishu. Eventually two of the ships spent a total of 14 days in two separate port areas before finally returning to their base at Diego Garcia. They had been gone a month but never unloaded their cargo.

What is most troubling for the future is that these problems took place in an environment that was austere but not the scene of active combat operations. This example emphasizes as few other aspects of the deployment the importance of integrating those things that must work together effectively:

- Timely intelligence on the port and its

characteristics
  • Current, well-informed assessments of its operational capacity
  • Deployment of transportation specialists so that they and their equipment arrive prior to the ships
  • Above all, a clear delineation of authority within the Joint Task Force to clarify who is in charge of making these things happen—and in time to make a difference.

Administrative Requirements

Lesson

  • **Peace operations impose their own unique administrative requirements that, like other aspects of the operation, must be managed effectively.**

Examples

One of the most persistent administrative problems throughout operations in Somalia was the lack of an efficient means to track funding and other costs of the operation, especially the supplies and services provided to coalition partners. Some of these requests for support involved strategic lift into the country while others concerned consumables such as water and rations. The absence of prior guidance and incomplete authority created an administrative burden that was only overcome with the usual work-arounds by dedicated people. Lessening those burdens in the future as we operate with reduced funding will require tighter financial controls (including those involving reimbursement) before a peace operation begins.

Procurement was also an issue. As had been the case with *Desert Storm*, there was an urgent need to have contracting officers on site early—and with authority sufficient to the monumental tasks of arranging for supplies and services that often had to be contracted in neighboring countries. During *Provide Relief* a request forwarded for the use of simplified contracting procedures during an operational contingency was turned down on the odd grounds that bullets were not being fired at U.S. forces by a declared enemy of the United States—this despite the fact that "imminent danger" pay had been approved for all U.S. forces operating in Somalia. During UNOSOM II, the U.N. logistical system came in for particular criticism. As one JULLS report stated:

> The U.N. procurement system is cumbersome, inefficient, and not suited to effectively support operations in an austere environment. The United Nations acquires all of its goods and services on a reimbursable basis. Unfortunately, the reimbursement is often delayed or debated, with a final solution that may not . . . benefit the provider.

Two joint issues that arose during *Restore Hope* were finance support and personnel rotation policies. Although pay operations are centralized in the Defense Finance & Accounting Service, the Navy and Marine Corps communicate this information through a single system used both on shore and during operational deployments. The

Army and Air Force lacked a comparable communications channel, a situation that caused some difficulties during the early stages of the *Restore Hope* and also demonstrated the need for such essential combat support systems to be deployable worldwide. Naturally, financial specialists trained to function in a joint environment are the basic underpinnings of any such system. Most of the personnel deployed during this operation were serving in a temporary duty status, a fact that led to confusion because of the wide differences in their tour lengths. Because a uniform policy was never established by either CENTCOM or the JTF, replacing personnel became a much more difficult task. Even more important was the potential morale problem inherent in having people serving side-by-side who had different tour lengths.

During *Restore Hope*, much of the Marine amphibious unit as well as most of the multinational contingent were quartered in and around the boundaries of the Mogadishu International Airport. Despite the fact that a comprehensive site plan had been prepared in advance of this occupation, it quickly broke down when different national contingents were added to the coalition. Because many of these countries provided only small units, there was no alternative except to house them at the airfield, so that encampments were soon claimed on a first-come, first-served basis. Apart from the inherent organizational problems stemming from such an approach, safety suffered as well when the encampments soon consumed all available space and spread toward taxiways, ramps, and active runways. Air controllers lived in tents sandwiched between the edge of the runway and high-powered

Marines deployed in support of Operation Restore Hope arrive at Mogadishu Airport on civilian aircraft.

area surveillance radars. When all other real estate had been claimed, an Army evacuation hospital more than lived up to its name when it was forced to set up just next to the end of the departure runway. The result was that, in an already threatening environment, there was needless exposure of the troops to a number of additional hazards.

Conduct of Operations

The operations conducted in Somalia during all three phases of the operation showed once again the true professionalism of the American soldier, sailor, airman, and marine. In all too many instances, Somalia showed as well the heroism and dedication of a force that found itself in harm's way while serving in the cause of peace. The full story of those operations and their significance at unit level is best left to the individual service components. The joint world as it affected the operations in Somalia dealt much more with the five areas presented here: command and control, mission execution, civil-military operations, negotiations, and intelligence.

Command and Control
Lessons

• It is a basic fact of life that the command and control of a coalition must always take into account the existence of parallel lines of authority, especially when the mission of the coalition involves combat.

• The basic doctrinal principles that govern U.S.

command relationships are appropriate for peace operations—and should have been applied in Somalia.

Examples

The major lessons on command and control that emerged from our operations in Somalia are instructive for what they reveal of problems both in coalition operations as well as in the U.S. chain of command put in place during UNOSOM II. That mission had barely begun before full-scale fighting flared up in Mogadishu and elsewhere in the countryside, leading to increased tactical challenges that in turn caused two major problems. Because the UNOSOM II headquarters was neither organized nor equipped to function as a battle staff, it had to undergo wrenching adjustments under great pressure. Even more seriously, however, the greater potential for combat increased the concern in those countries that had contributed forces to what they had originally seen as a humanitarian effort.

This concern manifested itself in a pronounced tendency for some of these national contingents to seek guidance from their respective capitals before carrying out even routine tactical orders. According to published reports, the commander of the Italian contingent went so far as to open separate negotiations with the fugitive warlord Mohammed Aideed—apparently with the full approval of his home government. With American backing, the United Nations requested this officer's relief from command for insubordination. The Italian Government refused and life went on—a useful demonstration of both the fundamental existence of parallel lines of authority and the fundamental difficulties of commanding a coalition force under combat conditions.

The escalating level of violence also caused additional command and control problems for the United States. As shown in figure 3, these arrangements were highly unusual. The logistical components of U.S. Forces in Somalia (USFORSOM) were OPCON (i.e., under operational control as "leased" forces) to the United Nations (in the person of MG Montgomery) while the QRF was still commanded and controlled (i.e., as COCOM or "owned" forces) by CENTCOM. MG Montgomery exercised his authority through an equally unusual combination of direct support, operational control, and tactical control. These command relationships were unusual but reflected three fundamental American objectives for UNOSOM II: to keep U.S. forces firmly under U.S. operational control, to reduce the visibility of U.S. combat forces in the operation, and to eliminate any misperception that those forces were under the command of the United Nations.

With the ever-deepening hunt for Aideed and the increasing involvement of the QRF in combat operations, the decision to deploy Task Force Ranger added an additional complicating factor. Because it was a strategic asset, Task Force Ranger had its own chain of command that was headed in country by Army Major General William F. Garrison and extended directly back to CENTCOM without going through either U.S. or U.N. channels. Although MG Montgomery did not have OPCON of this force, he maintained a close working relationship that allowed tight coordination between Task Force Ranger operations and the QRF. Because the QRF was under the direct tactical control of MG Montgomery and—because of its capabilities and the need to follow strict operational security procedures—it was normally designated as the back-up contingency force whenever Task Force Ranger went into action.

These same operational security concerns were apparently at the heart of MG Montgomery's request to add armor capabilities to the QRF from U.S. sources rather than relying on those already available from the coalition partners in Somalia. Although this request represented a clear signal that the level of violence was escalating yet again, there was no comprehensive reassessment of the mission at the national level. Instead, MG Montgomery's request for armor support was refused in a decision that has received wide public attention in light of the fateful Ranger operation that took place on the night of 3-4 October 1993. When the Rangers came under intense hostile fire, it rapidly became clear that the QRF lacked the capability to rescue them.

MG Montgomery and his staff reacted to that situation by quickly organizing an extraction force using Malaysian and Pakistani units equipped with tanks and armored personnel carriers—much as any U.S. commander in more conventional circumstances might have done in committing his reserves. However, the most important lesson to be drawn from these events may be the useful reminder that command and control ultimately rests upon the judgment of the on-scene commander and his ability to react to the unexpected.

In the aftermath of this battle, the United States decided to send additional troops to Somalia for additional protection of American forces. While this force was placed under U.S. command as a JTF, figure 5 shows how an already complicated command structure became still more complex. To illustrate (using only the basic acronyms)— the new JTF-Somalia fell under OPCON of CENTCOM but was TACON to USFORSOM. The purpose of this arrangement, in theory, was to allow the JTF Commander to concentrate on tactical missions while MG Montgomery was left free to concentrate on his responsibilities as the Deputy U.N. commander. Although the JTF thus controlled all U.S. tactical forces in Somalia neither the JTF nor USFORSOM controlled the Navy and Marine Corps forces, since those offshore assets were still under the operational control of CENTCOM. The JTF could not routinely task the offshore forces for such things as drone aircraft, although they did obtain Marine and SEAL sniper teams through an informal "handshake arrangement."

MG Montgomery has pointed out that many of these odd procedures were offset by the close working relationships he enjoyed with all U.S. commanders tasked to support UNOSOM II, and that "Ultimately the U.S. arrangements did work." That undeniable fact is yet another tribute to the dedication and professionalism of those charged with commanding and carrying out a difficult

FIGURE 5. *USFORSOM structure, October 1993*

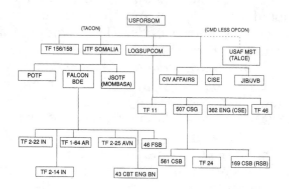

mission. *However, there should be no mistaking the fact that the greatest obstacles to unity of command during UNOSOM II were imposed by the United States on itself.* Especially at the end of the operation, these command arrangements had effectively created a condition that allowed no one to set clear, unambiguous priorities in designing and executing a comprehensive force package. Instead, CENTCOM exercised long-distance control over a number of organizationally co-equal entities in a remote theater of operations. As a UNOSOM II after-action report summed matters up:

> Unity of command and simplicity remain the key principles to be considered when designing a JTF command architecture. The warfighting JTF

commander must retain operational control of all forces available to him in theater and be allowed to posture those forces as allowed under UNAAF doctrine.

UNAAF doctrine is, of course, contained in Joint Pub. 0-2, which succinctly addresses the need for unity of command and simple, unambiguous command arrangements as a prerequisite for any military operation—but particularly for those involving joint and combined forces. The record of UNOSOM II suggests that peace operations should not be exempted from those standards. As a practical matter, it may also be useful to begin the planning for such operations with four basic questions:

- **Who shall command?**
- **With what forces?**
- **By what means?**
- **To what ends?**

To the extent that we are unable in future operations to answer those questions in simple terms, difficulties similar to UNOSOM II may once again await us.

Mission Execution

Lessons

- **Mission execution is more difficult without trained and well-organized staffs, especially in the joint environment of peace operations.**
- **Forcible disarmament is the "bright line" of peace operations: when you cross it, you have entered a de facto state of war.**

• **Restraint is an acquired skill, but it is the *sine qua non* of peace operations.**

Examples

The "standing-up" of JTF-Somalia in October 1993 provides a useful example of the continuing pitfalls of units entering a joint world for which they are not adequately prepared. Once again, this JTF was formed around a nucleus—this time the Army's 10th Mountain Division. Because of its tactical orientation, no division—and especially not a light infantry unit—has either the staff structure or the cadre of experienced personnel needed to conduct joint operations. Necessarily, staff procedures are "Army" rather than "joint". The kinds of communications and ADP equipment required to conduct joint operations are also missing in these divisions. What made matters worse was that, in spite of these anomalies, the division was given the JTF mission and accepted the handoff for that responsibility in Somalia *less than 2 weeks after receipt of the warning order.*

Other misconceptions included the assumption that the JTF staff could be "small," or that one of the division's brigades could function effectively as a de facto Army component command. And although the officer placed in command of the JTF was an Army officer, Major General Carl F. Ernst, he had not previously been assigned to the division—a fact that made the establishment of new working relationships another burden among many. The fact that the division acquitted itself well under these demanding circumstances owed much not only to its superb personnel but also to the fact that the mission was largely confined to force protection for the balance of its in-country tour.

If there was a critical difference between the specific tasks during the final two phases of the operation, it was that the security and peacekeeping functions typical of *Restore Hope* (patrolling, mine clearance, heavy weapons confiscation) became indistinguishable from normal combat operations during UNOSOM II. MG Montgomery may have said it best: "If this isn't combat, then I'm sure having a helluva nightmare." Unlike the well-organized nucleus of the Marine headquarters in charge of UNITAF, the execution of more demanding missions during UNOSOM II became even more difficult because the Force Command headquarters was not equipped to act like a battle staff. The initial difficulties in manning this headquarters were never entirely overcome, with the result that key functions—long-range supporting fires, combat engineers, and air operations—were either missing or not available 24 hours a day. The JTF had to improvise a Joint Operations Center using existing equipment and personnel, many of whom had no real expertise in some of the areas for which they were now responsible: joint and combined ground operations, fire support, air operations, training, and intelligence. Equally important was the need to institute effective means for liaison with adjacent multinational commands. While hard work and rapid adaptation clearly helped, it is difficult in these stressful situations to link current operations with future operations—and both of these with overall mission requirements.

That need is nowhere greater than in peace operations, and here, too, there was a contrast between *Restore Hope* and UNOSOM II on the all-important issue of disarmament. While their different approaches to some extent reflected different missions, the UNITAF leadership was reluctant to do more than to confiscate those weapons that threatened his force and its mission, for example, "technicals" and weapons caches. The more ambitious UNOSOM II disarmament mission—although it never became more than an incidental byproduct of the Aideed manhunt—was a direct threat to the position of the clans within the local power structure and was resisted accordingly. The respective difficulties of executing these two missions should consequently serve as a "bright line on the ground" in planning future peace operations. There is a basic conceptual difference between arms control and disarmament. Removing or limiting the major weapons of an inferior or defeated military force can be thought of as a form of arms control, *but to commit military forces to the mission of forcibly disarming a populace is to commit those forces to a combat situation that may thereafter involve them as an active belligerent.*

Ambassador Robert B. Oakley, President Bush's Special Envoy to Somalia, pointed out that the application of force imposes special challenges for peacekeepers who wish to avoid becoming active belligerents. This challenge involves a mindset that looks at the local populace as potential allies rather than likely enemies, that gives repeated warningsbefore the application of force against any hostile act; that limits the application of force to the minimum level required, and that constantly seeks to engage in a dialogue rather than being tricked into overreaction. U.S. forces throughout the operations in Somalia clearly did their best to follow that advice before the UNOSOM II mandate

U.S. Marines commence a raid on Mogadishu's Bakara Market, in a raid for arms and munitions. One cache yielded enough to fill a 2.5-ton truck.

made many of those points moot. Even then, American forces were under standing orders to limit civilian casualties and collateral damage. According to General Montgomery, for example, 15-minute, 10-minute, and 5-minute warnings were normally given before attacking any target. Although the use of AC-130 gunships, helicopter rockets, and Ranger raids over the streets of Mogadishu clearly conveyed other messages to the media, some of the precise targetting procedures used as well as the constant search for more accurate, less deadly munitions represent significant steps to adapt military power to those situations where the line between combat and noncombat is difficult to draw.

Civil-Military Operations

Lessons

• The real "peacekeepers" in a peace operation are the humanitarian relief organizations (HRO's) that provide both aid for the present and hope for the future.

• The HRO's can be our allies, but they must at least be part of our planning and coordination efforts.

Examples

Although the civil affairs officer is a familiar participant in many military operations, there was no doctrine in the collective experiences of either the services or the Joint Staff to cover a situation in which a country had descended into a state of anarchy. Along the way, however, there was a rediscovery of the need to consider military, diplomatic, and humanitarian efforts as parts of a common whole. Although there was no longer a single government in Somalia, there were at least 49 different international agencies, including U.N. bodies, nongovernmental organizations, and HRO's. Dealing effectively with those agencies became the primary challenge for civil-military operations in Somalia. This was an important function because the HRO's not only provided many of the relief supplies that helped fight starvation, but agencies such as the Red Cross and Feed the Children were on the scene prior to the arrival of our forces and long after their departure. To this basic difference in perspective should be added another: for a variety of reasons, relief agencies tend to be suspicious of military and security personnel, even when they come as peacekeepers.

Women and children line up for a meal at a feeding center run by the Irish humanitarian aid group Concern in the village of Waine Wein, Somalia.

One thing that affected relations in Somalia was the pattern of accommodation that the relief agencies had followed to ensure they could work there effectively. This usually meant hiring local security forces—often in concert with the area's dominant clan. When peacekeeping forces arrived to set up their own security arrangements, there were the inevitable questions as to their authority. Once these issues were settled, it was also necessary to make exceptions to policy when weapons were confiscated from those people employed by the relief organizations as their security forces.

During the UNITAF phase of the operation there was an undeniable increase in both security and the amount of relief supplies being distributed. This period of relative peace allowed more relief agencies to enter the country, but it also underlined the need to insure closer civil-military cooperation. Sometimes these cooperative efforts involved small but important things—such as allowing HRO representatives to fly "space available" on military aircraft. More substantial efforts took place when military forces during both *Restore Hope* and UNOSOM II worked side by side with relief agencies to dig wells, rebuild roads, repair schools, and the like. With the need to control access to key port areas and food distribution points, it also became essential to provide photo ID cards to the relief workers. This requirement in turn meant setting up procedures for verifying organizational and personal *bona fides* because, as one observer said, "People came to view the ID card as both official UNITAF certification of a person's role as a humanitarian worker and also as a gun permit." Finally, some agency had to issue the cards and to regulate what privileges, if any, these ID cards would convey.

A Somali boy has taken the Somali fascination for glasses one step further by crafting a pair for himself out of a discarded shower shoe.

For these and similar reasons, one of the most important initiatives of the Somalia operation was the establishment of the Civil-Military Operations Center (CMOC). Set up in December 1992 during the early stages of UNITAF, CMOC became the key coordinating point between the task force and the HRO's. Liaison officers from the major multinational contingents, together with the U.S. command, used this center as a means of coordinating their activities—such as providing military support for convoys of relief supplies and assigning pier space and port access to Mogadishu Harbor for the HRO's. These practical duties also lent themselves to the broadening of contacts between the military and civilian components, including the creation of parallel CMOC's in each of the nine Humanitarian Relief Sectors. Eventually, CMOC controlled the issue of ID cards and maintained a data matrix showing the status of food relief supplies throughout the command's area of operations. Equally important, however, was the fact that CMOC was able to work closely with the

U.S. trucks filled with medical personnel and medicine line the streets of Mogadishu to perform the first medical civic action program in Somalia.

Humanitarian Operations Center run by the United Nations—thus allowing a single focal point for all relief agencies operating in-country. The staff of CMOC was deliberately kept small in order to keep it focused on its mission of coordination and information exchange. (This innovation is sufficiently important as a precedent for the future;

its table of organization and principal functions are summarized in appendix C.)

Negotiations

Lesson

At all levels during Somalia operations, negotiating skills and techniques were essential to mission accomplishment. As Marine Corps Lieutenant General Anthony Zinni said, "Always consider negotiations as a great alternative to violence."

Examples

Joint Pub 3-07.3 notes that, in addition to the qualities of patience and restraint, peacekeepers must combine

> an approachable, understanding, and tactful manner with fairness and firmness. A professional demeanor that stresses quiet diplomacy and reasoning will achieve more than arrogance, anger, disdain, coercion, or sarcasm. Personnel must be able to cope positively when each side seeks to press its position and then reacts vocally when stopped.

These qualities are clearly part of an attitude adjustment from the reactions traditionally associated with military operations: but there should be no mistaking how important that adjustment is during peace operations.

One perspective was offered by MG Montgomery, who noted that "consensus building" was a critical part of the process of developing plans and preparing operations orders in any combined operation—not just those involving peace operations. During UNOSOM II, however, the specific terms of reference guiding the participation of each multinational contingent as well as their different views of employment doctrine meant that actions could not be taken without broad agreement. Finding those areas of consensus, building on them, and applying them to specific operations are inevitably complicated processes—and ones that are noticeably different form those that most military personnel are used to. However, MG Montgomery thought negotiating skills important enough to recommend that they be addressed at Army professional schools.

U.S.A.F. workers unload flour from a C-130 Hercules aircraft as Operation Restore Hope *workers begin another day of humanitarian relief efforts to Somalia.*

Another perspective comes from **Army Staff Sergeant Brian O'Keefe**, who served outside Mogadishu during *Restore Hope* and now trains soldiers in the peacekeeping skills he learned in that environment. An Army publication recently pointed out that he quickly came to realize that a "show the flag and kick ass" approach was not good enough. Instead, tact in applying ROE and weapons-confiscation policies was essential, as was the use of water bottles and smiles as basic negotiating tools. "Most of all, we learned what it takes to conduct peacekeeping operations: negotiating skills, patience, and a whole lot of common sense."

The fundamental importance of maintaining this kind of a dialogue led to a key UNITAF innovation: a "Combined Security Committee" that allowed LTG Johnston and key members of his staff to meet frequently with Mohammed Aideed and other key clan leaders. This forum proved especially useful in gaining and even forcing cooperation with UNITAF mandates, such as weapons cantonment. As LTG Johnston recounts the purpose of that dialogue:

> Aideed and Ali Mahdi were often unhappy with the message we would send from time to time, but for the most part (they) complied. *You may not like the characters you have to deal with but you are better able to uncover their motives and intentions if you keep a communications link open* (emphasis added).

Intelligence

Lessons

• **Intelligence is as vital to the success of a peace operation as it is to any other military activity.**

• **Although nonintrusive means of collecting information are especially useful for peace operations, human intelligence is usually the key.**

Examples

It has taken the United Nations several years of ever more intense involvement in complicated operations before it has quietly admitted something that military people have always known: intelligence is the key to any operation, including those designed to secure the peace. While "information," is the term of choice, operations in Somalia proved that, whatever it is called, intelligence has a crucial role to play at the lower end of the conflict spectrum as well as in other places. A wide range of intelligence systems was employed there, many of them for the first time. Night-vision devices, ground-surveillance radars, tactical air reconnaissance, and unmanned aerial vehicles all played important roles in providing tactical intelligence and early-warning information. The most basic intelligence in a low-intensity conflict scenario is invariably provided by humans, the best and most important HUMINT source always being the soldier or marine in the field. Patrol tactics and intelligence requirements were adjusted to allow his eyes and ears to provide U.S. commanders with better "situation awareness."

The major problems encountered came in two categories. There is always an issue of how to pipe intelligence from national sources down to the on-scene commander—but this was so difficult in a country with no functioning telephone system that all the links had to be provided by satellite. To provide a focal point for dissemination, CENTCOM established an Intelligence Support Element (ISE) staffed solely by U.S. personnel. The ISE rapidly became the single most important part of the intelligence support to UNOSOM—which raised the second problem. U.S. law expressly forbids dissemination through any intelligence channel over which there is anything other than exclusive U.S. control. In addition, there was great concern that sensitive U.S. intelligence sources and methods might be compromised in the setting of multinational operations. For both these reasons, guidelines were developed and adhered to which limited the dissemination of information relating to targetting and operational security but generally permitted the flow of timely intelligence to the coalition. U.S. officers serving in the UNOSOM Force Command Staff normally acted as the conduit for information developed by the ISE in support of specific operations—with MG Montgomery often making the final call on its dissemination. In all cases, however, LTG Bir as the Force Commander was kept fully apprised of the complete U.S. intelligence picture as it affected his area of operations.

If there is a precedent for the future it is that peace operations present a new kind of "information war" in which the side with the best situation awareness has a great edge—and in a multinational setting there are, by definition, many sides. While intelligence has traditionally tended to focus on the enemy, the definition of who or what the enemy is in a peace operation is not always clear. Clearly the forces of Mohammed Aideed became the main adversary that the U.S. had to contend with in Somalia. In future operations, however, commanders may want to gear their intelligence and other information collection systems—including the front-line soldier—to collect as well on those indicators signalling the direction in which the operation is heading. The use of CMOC to monitor the status of food distribution in Somalia from all relief agencies is one example of the creative use of information to build better situational awareness through the use of nontraditional mission indicators. Future operations may suggest others.

Support

The unprecedented nature of the operations in Somalia created a new range of problems for the critical support services that must work effectively if the mission is to be successful. There was no telephone service of any kind, and such logistical facilities as there were resembled those of a war zone—yet the troops had to be supported, an infrastructure hastily constructed, and the American people kept informed of what their sons and daughters were doing in this singularly inhospitable climate. Here again, the key factor in adapting to these challenges was the quality of the joint force serving in Somalia.

Communications and Interoperability

Lessons

- **In a peace operation, the inherent difficulties of command and control demand effective communications among the strategic, operational, and tactical levels.**
- **Diverse coalition forces generally mean wildly different communications capabilities—a fact of life that demands effective communications management.**

Examples

Operation *Provide Relief* entered an environment in which there were few, if any, communications pathways between the strategic and forward-operating base. The baseline communications capabilities they brought with them are summarized in figure 6; such packages may well serve as models for the future.

During both *Restore Hope* and UNOSOM II, the communications support provided to U.S. forces was generally superb, with "connectivity" helping to overcome some of the inherent difficulties of ensuring that unity of effort, if not command, was being exercised. Part of what made this system work was the presence of a liaison officer from the Defense Information Systems Agency to UNITAF at the very start of the operation, an arrangement that permitted some flexibility in adjusting communications packages and pathways. The

FIGURE 6. *Baseline communications requirements for humanitarian assistance missions*

- DSN (GMF Suite)
- Autodin (GMF Suite/Tactical Comm Center)
- Intra-camp Telephone System (tactical switchboard; phones; at least 2 STU-III's)
- Facsimile machines (secure and nonsecure)
- Secure Tactical Satellite Radio (UHF TACSAT)
- Long-Range UHF Radio (MRC-138 or equivalent)
- Commercial Satellite Terminal (INMARSAT)
- Support Items: cables, generators
- Others: handheld radios; public address systems, copiers, extra batteries, diskettes, computer paper

operation utilized both military and commercial satellite linkages, although the availability and efficiency of the commercial INMARSAT telephone service were offset somewhat by the fact that it cost $6 a minute. Another problem was that the popularity of this system quickly outran its capacity. Because this and other communication pathways became crowded, even an austere signalling environment rapidly became crowded and required increasing attention to the "de-confliction" of radio frequencies being used by the military units and HRO's.

The size of the operating area also stretched in-country communications. Infantry units commonly operated more than 50 miles from their headquarters, while transportation and engineer units were often hundreds of miles from their bases. Either HF or TACSAT were potential answers, but both the equipment and the available net structures were limited. The operations provided a number of opportunities to experiment with tactical satellite antennaes, especially those that could provide continuous communications—and better force protection—for convoys operating in remote, high-threat areas. Soldiers at all levels repeated the experience of *Desert Storm* and brought their personal computers with them—especially the newer laptop versions. Field expedients flourished to protect them from blowing wind and sand—including the taping of Ziplock baggies across the opening to the disk drive in a way that allowed access to the floppy disk but effectively sealed out dust.

The most significant potential for interoperability problems occurred between U.S. forces and the multinational contingents. During UNITAF, these problems were minimized by two important expedients: imposing communications management discipline over the force as a whole; and assigning full-time liaison officers with tactical satellite radios to each of the multinational contingents—much as had been done during the Gulf War. During UNOSOM II, however, and with the U.S. no longer in charge, those practices were discontinued. Instead, each tactical area of responsibility was commanded by one of the multinational contingents, whose comanders were responsible for ensuring that all forces under their operational control had compatible communications equipment. Because area boundaries roughly corresponded to national forces, this system worked reasonably well—as long as each national force stuck to its own area. Crossing over the "seams" of national control created severe interoperability problems—a situation that occurred whenever one national contingent had to cross over an area boundary to reinforce another.

Some of these problems had been offset earlier by the operational communications structure set up and manned by UNITAF. Following the Marine redeployment, a backbone communications capability from the 11th Signal Brigade was maintained in each of the areas of operation until a U.N. structure was established in December 1993. However, other communications responsibilities were effectively turned over to the signal battalion of the Army's 10th Mountain Division. There is, unfortunately, no way that a division-level signal battalion could be prepared to assume what amounted to a strategic communications mission, especially one in which so many different communications systems were being used.

The internal interoperability problems affecting affected U.S. forces did not involve any Grenada-like operational fiascoes; however, the ones that did occur underline the continuing problem of aligning equipment, procedures, and standards in the joint environment. During *Restore Hope*, it was discovered that UNITAF, as a Marine-centered headquarters, used an obscure word-processing software called Enable OA, while CENTCOM, like most other military users, preferred Wordperfect. A similar difficulty plagued their exchanges of e-mail.

U.S. Army UH-60 Blackhawk helicopter lands at the Belet Uen airstrip, dropping off soldiers from 2nd Brigade, 10th Mountain Division, Fort Drum, NY, to seize the airstrip as part of a combined U.S. and Canadian assault during Operation Restore Hope.

This situation complicated, although it did not prevent, file transfers between the two headquarters; however, it illustrates the growing importance of "officeware" in military operations and the problems resulting from mismatches. In the tactical arena, it was also discovered that the air-tasking order formats differed between the east and west coast ships of the Marine Amphibious Ready Groups—and that the same Army and Marine single-channel tactical radios had acquired compatibility problems caused by differing upgrades. Most seriously, for the first 3 weeks the Navy was offshore, the Army hospital in Mogadishu could not talk to the ships, nor were Army MEDEVAC helicopter pilots cleared to land on them.

All these and many other difficulties were overcome by capable, problem-solving people. The more difficult and much longer term issue is the "stovepiping" of different data systems. During *Restore Hope* there were at least 10 different data systems, most built around the requirements of a single service but handling a host of common functions: intelligence, personnel, logistics, finance, etc. Each system brought its own logistical "tail" and required its own lane on the very narrow information highway available to deployed forces. This is not a situation that makes sense from either a logistical or operational perspective. One after action report summarized the problem:

> Time spent trying to learn and engineer just the (comparatively) few systems we were associated with during Restore Hope could have been better spent providing higher quality, overall service. Money spent on these circuits could have gone a long way to resolving our interoperability problems.

In-Country Logistics

a. Lesson

We have the finest theater-level combat service support organization in the world: it will be either sought after or modelled in any future peace operation.

Examples

The "lessons learned" from the performance of the combat service support structure in Somalia do not so much suggest the need for specific corrections as much as they underline the importance of the U.S. contribution to the success of this or any future peace operation. What is clear especially from the record of our support to UNOSOM II is that the management of theater-level combat service support in an austere environment is something in which we excel. The basic concept for UNOSOM was that support functions would be organized around the U.N. Logistics Support Command (UNLSC)—a structure that closely and deliberately resembled an Army Corps Support Group.

This command was augmented by U.S. logistics personnel as well as task-organized units from the smaller national contingents. Although the terms of reference for each member of the multinational contingent specified the types of support they would give and receive, the general rule was that the UNLSC would provide common user items (such as fuel and water) while the national contingents supplied their own specific needs (ammunition and maintenance). In practice, however, the wide variations in the equipment brought by the national contingents meant that there was a constant competition for resources, with the United States often making up the difference. As the operation progressed into more intense combat, and with correspondingly greater logistical demands, the presumption of self-sufficiency broke down more and more. Although such responsibilities had never been intended, this small logistical force eventually provided both general support and direct support to a large portion of the coalition. The resulting demands on both the U.N. logistics structure and its American underpinnings were intense—and accomplished only by the extraordinary efforts of U.S. logistical personnel. As both history and precedent, there is little question that the logistical ability the U.S. displayed in Somalia will either be requested or copied in all future peace operations.

Medical

Lesson

In peace operations, especially multinational ones, it is essential that medical support personnel come prepared to deal with some of the world's most deadly and exotic diseases.

Examples

The United States has had significant experience in coping with the challenges of medical care in austere environments. What made Somalia unique was that there were literally no host country hospital facilities to augment those that the United States was prepared to bring. One lesson from that experience is that it will be useful in the future to track medical facilities theaterwide, as well as countrywide. As an example, it became necessary to arrange for the evacuation of U.S. personnel to neighboring Kenya and their treatment there.

Another point is that medical intelligence is crucial

in helping prevent exposure to indigenous diseases. In Somalia, earthmoving equipment brought in to repair roads and other facilities released tuberculosis spores long dormant in the soil. An additional problem to be faced was that the full range of expertise in tropical medicine was required, to help treat the medical problems not only of the indigenous population but those of the multinational contingents as well. Although the United States may not be directly responsible for these personnel, it is probably inevitable that we will be expected to give some form of medical support to future coalition partners.

Media

Lesson

An effective public information program is critical to the success of any operation, especially those involving peacemaking or peacekeeping.

Examples

The lessons learned from Somalia about military relations with the media suggest the importance of two things:

• First, there must be an efficient means of dealing with visitors, including not only the media but congressional leaders and other public figures. The horror of the suffering in Somalia as well as the role of American forces in an entirely new operational setting were bound to attract such attention—and did so consistently. Most public affairs operations in the military are well equipped to handle such duties, but planning for their employment in peace operations should not be left to chance. In fact, a good rule may be to have the public affairs team on the first plane in country.

• The second point is the importance of information. If the mission has been well analyzed, the correct milestones chosen, and the means of collecting the appropriate indicators determined, the leadership will have an effective degree of situation awareness. The commander's ability to communicate that situational awareness to the media (as well as the chain of command) is a real test of leadership. How well the public information officer defines that situation in every public comment, TV appearance, or newspaper interview will similarly help to determine how the mission is perceived at the tactical, operational, and strategic levels. The uncomfortable glare of the media spotlight is a necessary part of the consensus-building process which, as MG Montgomery pointed out, is an intrinsic part of combined operations in any multinational setting. As usual, this was a lesson learned the hard way:

> U.S. forces in UNOSOM II had no public affairs organization. And one of the major lessons learned is that any U.S. force which is part of a U.N. operation must have a first class public affairs section in the future. After 3 October I was sent a 30-man Joint Information Bureau— and quality of coverage improved enormously thereafter.

The responsibility of sharing situational awareness with the media is a basic and most important function in an age where information especially affects those military activities carried out with the concurrence of the international community. In our system, however, the media spotlight serves the additional purpose of public accountability and highlights our special responsibilities whenever we put the lives of American troops at risk—something that is an inevitable part of any peace operation.

III. CONCLUSIONS

The difference between genius and stupidity is that genius has limits.

Anonymous

The basic challenge confronting those who commit U.S. forces to peace operations is knowing how to get them in effectively when the situation warrants—and how to get them out once their mission has been accomplished. While recognizing the importance of "perseverance" in operations other than war, the real test of this principle is to ensure that the United States remains able to project its power when needed—and avoids indefinite commitments at the expense of its other responsibilities worldwide. By itself, our operations in Somalia did not seriously interfere with those reponsibilities, but the record of our intervention into that most unfortunate country teaches us that there must be limits to the commitment of American military power. That experience also suggests the existence of certain "bright lines" in peace operations indicating when those limits are being reached. *One of them involves the use of military forces in nation-building, a mission for which our forces should not be primarily responsible.* While military power may well set the stage for such action, the real responsibility for

89

nation-building must be carried out by the civilian agencies of the government better able to specialize in such long-term humantiarian efforts. Another "bright line" is any action in a peace operation that effectively takes sides between factions engaged in internal civil strife—clearly as much of a problem for U.S. troops in Somali as it was for an earlier generation of American soldiers in the Dominican Republic and Lebanon. Such actions certainly include coercive disarmament of a populace, an act that is qualitatively different from simply controlling or confiscating the arms which may overtly threaten the peacekeeping force. The reason: In societies where peacekeeping may be needed, the distribution of arms reflects internal power structures (political, cultural, ethnic or even tribal) that can be expected to fight to maintain their position. *If the disarmament of the population becomes an objective, then there should be no mistaking the fact that the troops given this mission have been committed to combat.*

The uncertainties surrounding the Somalia operations also underline the importance of understanding the strengths and limitations of the United Nations and other international institutions. In the case of the United Nations, this means ensuring that its mandates are precise and fully reflect a clear understanding of a given situation and its military implications. The importance of this principle cannot be understated; the Somalia experience shows just how directly the changing mandates of the United Nations shaped the different missions of the military forces sent there. Future American policymakers familiar with this record will have strong incentives to ensure that changes in any future U.N. mandate are fully reconciled with the specific military capabilities required to execute them. That experience suggests as well why the Presidential Directive of May 1994 stated that U.N. command would not be the tool of choice in future peace enforcement operations. The larger point here, however, is not whether U.S. soldiers should serve under U.N. control: *No soldiers of any nationality should be expected to serve under the U.N. command structure in any combat setting until the reforms called for by the President in PDD-25 have been put in place.* At a minumum, such reforms must achieve more effective means than those demonstrated in Somalia for commanding, controlling, coordinating, and communicating with multinational forces committed to peace operations.

These limitations should not blind us, however, to the great strengths which U.N. agencies and humanitarian relief organizations bring to the international arena. Some of the most valuable contributions by U.S. and coalition troops in Somalia were digging the wells, grading the roads, and working side by side with many of the agencies listed in appendix B, agencies that are the real peacekeepers and peacebuilders. But we should understand that their perspectives reflect permanent commitments, while military perspectives are necessarily shorter. Even more important is the recognition that the careful integration of diplomatic and military activities with humanitarian actions not only contributes to the overall success of the mission but also reduces the potential for casualties.

The need to work effectively with coalition partners also highlights the difficulty of exercising unity of command in anything like the classic sense. Unity of effort, or at least unity of purpose, is a more realistic goal in coalition operations—as it has been since the Peloponnesian Wars. However, there is no reason why we should settle for anything less than unity of command over the American forces that may be committed to peace operations or, for that matter, any other joint operation. The three chains of command running during UNOSOM II underline the importance of a lesson that should be adapted from Murphy's Laws of Combat: *If it takes more than 10 seconds to explain the command arrangements, they probably won't work.*

The way in which command was structured by the U.S. forces sent to Somalia also deserves some careful attention in the future because of the persistent problems in organizing joint task forces. While there is lively debate about whether the unified commands should organize "standing joint task forces," there should now be little doubt that the organization of the headquarters for those task forces is an issue that should no longer be left to last-minute arrangements. More specifically, it helps if any joint headquarters is built around a nucleus of people already accustomed to working together, and it helps even more if that nucleus reflects solid expertise in joint and combined operations. There should be no question that developing and broadening this expertise is a fundamental requirement for the American military establishment. During UNOSOM II, for example, U.S. forces were also engaged in *12 other major operations* requiring the formation of joint task forces—operations ranging from patrolling no-fly zones over Iraq to providing flood relief in the American Midwest. Far from being unusual or extraordinary events, it should be recognized that the formation of joint task forces has now become "business as usual" for the Armed Forces of the United States.

Another basic insight coming out of the Somalia experience is that the new emphasis on peace operations has not rescinded the fundamentals of military operations. As always those missions must begin with a strategy that focuses on long-term interests. The lack of a consistent "big picture" focus was clearly one of the things that complicated the transitions between the various phases of the operation—the relative success of UNITAF making the task of UNOSOM II more difficult. Equally fundamental military tasks are those that must be developed from a clear strategy: mission analysis and operations plans leading to clearly defined objectives. While those tasks were certainly undertaken in Somalia, the record of what we did there also contains a clear warning for the future: *Beware of the temptation to do too much.*

Giving in to that temptation is an occupational hazard in an institution built around can-do attitudes and the expectation of success. All the more reason, then, to insure that the analysis of any peace operation includes the selection of those indicators that can best measure mission accomplishment. What signs, for example, would show if the levels of violence were increasing or decreasing? How should these things be measured and by what part of the command? Such an unconventional approach to mission analysis may also help to focus on something clearly missing in Somalia—emphasizing single operations rather than focussing on the continuity of the mission as a whole from the overriding perspective of U.S. interests. It is this perspective that should guide the determination of entry and exit strategies, as well as fix our position at any moment on the line between them.

Three other issues arise from the Somalia experience that may have equally lasting significance because they show how U.S. military power is adjusting to the realities of the post-Cold War world:

• In deployment patterns, for example, we have long excelled at quickly moving large numbers of forces, supplies, and equipment overseas—precisely as we would have done in the event of a NATO reinforcement. In peace operations, especially those where the major function is disaster relief or humanitarian aid, we will certainly need to be able to fine tune those deployments. Rather than massive airlifts, for example, it may make more sense to put a future JTF commander in on the ground as early as possible and allow him to tailor the package as needed. This will certainly mean adjusting JOPES and TPFDD procedures to allow the additional flexibility. Conversely, it will also mean even greater emphasis on user discipline, because JOPES, in particular, is the common link among the CINC, the components, the supporting commands, and the deploying forces.

- The second issue is the understanding of the world at large that the professional military brings to its preparations for operations ranging from peacekeeping to general war. It used to be that most of this expertise was centered on the Soviet Union, Western Europe, or Korea, for obvious reasons. Now, however, the importance of more broadly focused "area studies" has increased, despite the fact that acquiring this expertise has not been a traditional milestone on the path to higher level command, advancement, and promotion. The Somalia experience underlines the importance of knowing the country, the culture, the ground, and the language as a pre-condition for military operations, with improvisations in this instance making notably good use of the expertise brought by Reserve Component personnel. Another recent example of the particular strengths of having a commander schooled in a local culture was provided by General Norman Schwarzkopf. Although his exposure to Middle Eastern culture came primarily from his boyhood experiences in the region, this expertise was especially valuable in leading the Gulf War coalition. Insuring as a matter of policy that the future officer corps will have similar strengths is an issue that must be carefully addressed within the military educational establishment.

- The third issue is one that is quickly summed up: Peace operations such as those in Somalia show how the training and professionalism of the men and women in our Armed Forces are as important in adapting to the requirements of new, nontraditional missions as they are in carrying out the demands of more conventional scenarios. For those forces likely to be deployed as peacekeepers, supplementary training is always a good idea—for situation-specific orientations, for familiarization with typical operational tasks, and especially for building the staff competencies required by joint or multinational environments.

There is, however, an important sense in which the most basic qualification of our Armed Forces to act as peacekeepers rests upon their credibility as warfighters. Their technical competence and physical prowess allow our soldiers, sailors, airmen, and marines to prevail in any operational environmental: but their record of going in harm's

way in the cause of peace is one that preceded our intervention in Somalia and that will endure long after the controversies surrounding it have faded. President Clinton surely spoke for the American people when he welcomed home the 10th Mountain Division after their redeployment from Somalia in March 1994:

> If there are any debates still to be had about our mission in Somalia, let people have those debates with me. But let there be no debate about how you carried out your mission. . . . You have shown the world what Americans are made of. Your nation is grateful and your President is terribly, terribly proud of you.

APPENDIX A:
Selected Bibliography

Listed below are publications developed by the Joint Staff and the military services that may assist the JTF Commander in operations like Somalia, where the environment is unpredictable, the operation falls in the category of "other than war," and there may be other agencies, nations, and private organizations involved. Publications still in draft form are nonetheless listed so the reader may watch for their publication.

Joint Publications

Joint Chiefs of Staff. *Joint Pub 1, "Joint Warfare of the US Armed Forces."* U.S. Government Printing Office, Washington, DC, 11 November 1991.

Joint Chiefs of Staff. *Joint Pub 0-2, "Unified Action Armed Forces (UNAAF)."* U.S. Government Printing Office, Washington, DC, 11 August 1994.

Joint Chiefs of Staff. *Joint Pub 3-0, "Doctrine for Joint Operations."* U.S. Government Printing Office, Washington, DC, 9 September 1993.

Joint Chiefs of Staff. *Joint Pub 3-07, "Joint Doctrine for Military Operations Other Than War."* (Draft)

Joint Chiefs of Staff. *Joint Pub 3-07.1, "Joint*

Tactics, Techniques, and Procedures for Foreign Internal Defense (FID)." U.S. Government Printing Office, Washington, DC, 20 December 1993.

Joint Chiefs of Staff. *Joint Pub 3-07.3, "Joint Tactics, Techniques, and Procedures for Peacekeeping Operations."* U.S. Government Printing Office, Washington, DC, 29 April 1994.

Joint Chiefs of Staff. *Joint Pub 3-07.6, "Joint Tactics, Techniques, and Procedures for Foreign Humanitarian Assistance."* (Draft)

Joint Chiefs of Staff. *Joint Pub 3-17, Joint Tactics Techniques and Procedures for Theater Airlift Operations."* (Draft) Joint Chiefs of Staff. *Joint Pub 5-00.2, "Joint Task Force Planning Guidance and Procedures."* U.S. Government Printing Office, Washington, DC, 3 September 1993.

Multi-Service Publications

Air Land Sea Application Center. *"Multi-Service Procedures for Humanitarian Assistance Operations."* (Draft) This publication is in development as of this writing. Each service will adopt it into their publications system upon completion.

U.S. Army Publications

Headquarters, Department of the Army. *Field Manual 7-98, "Operations in Low Intensity Conflict."* U.S. Government Printing Office, Washington, DC, 19 October 1992.

Headquarters, Department of the Army. *Field*

Manual 100-7, "Decisive Force: The Army in Theater Operations." (Final Draft)

Headquarters, Department of the Army. *Field Manual 100-8, "Multinational Army Operations."* (Final Draft)

Headquarters, Department of the Army. *Field Manual 100-16, "Army Operational Support."* (Final Draft)

Headquarters, Department of the Army. *Field Manual 100-23, "Peace Operations."* (Final Draft)

Center for Army Lessons Learned. *Handbook for the Soldier in Operations Other Than War (OOTW)."* U.S. Government Printing Office, Washington, DC, July 1994.

U.S. Navy Publications

Headquarters, Department of the Navy. *TACNOTE ZZ 0050.1.94, "Maritime Interception Operations."* U.S. Government Printing Office, Washington, DC, 1 July 1994.

Headquarters, Department of the Navy. TACMEMO XZ 0057.1.92, "Maritime Conduct of Noncombatant Evacuation Operations." (Draft) U.S. Government Printing Office, Washington, DC, 30 May 1993.

Headquarters, Department of the Navy. *TACMEMO XZ 0021.1.93, "Expeditionary Forces Conducting Humanitarian Assistance."* (Draft)

U. S. Marine Corps Publications

Headquarters, U.S. Marine Corps. *Fleet Marine Force Manual 1-5, "Maritime Prepositioned*

Shipping." U.S. Government Printing Office, Washington, DC, September 1993.

Headquarters, U.S. Marine Corps. *Fleet Marine Force Manual 1-23, "Forcible Entry Operations."* (Draft)

Headquarters, U.S. Marine Corps. *Fleet Marine Force Manual 4, "Combat Service Support."* U.S. Government Printing Office, Washington, DC, August 1993.

Headquarters, U.S. Marine Corps. *Operational Handbook 1-24, "Expeditionary Forces Conducting Humanitarian Assistance Missions."* U.S. Government Printing Office, Washington, DC, 1993.

U. S. Air Force Publications

Headquarters, U.S. Air Force. *Air Force Doctrine Directive 35, "Special Operations."* U.S. Government Printing Office, Washington, DC.

Headquarters, U.S. Air Force. *Air Force Doctrine Directive 3, "Military Operations Other Than War."* (Draft)

Headquarters, U.S. Air Force. *Air Force Doctrine Directive 12, "Airspace Control in a Combat Zone."* (Draft)

Headquarters, U.S. Air Force. *Air Force Doctrine Directive 30, "Airlift Operations."* (Draft)

Deputy Chief of Staff, Plans and Operations; Headquarters, U.S. Air Force. *JFACC Primer (Second Edition, February 1994).* HQ, USAF/XOXD, Washington, DC, February 1994.

National Defense University Publications

Although these NDU publications are not doctrinal in nature, they do contain information that is valuable to the operational commander.

Graham, James R., ed. *Non-Combat Roles for the U.S. Military in the Post-Cold War Era.* 1993.

Lewis, William H., ed. *Military Implications of United Nations Peacekeeping Operations.* June 1993.

Lewis, William H., ed. *Peacekeeping: The Way Ahead?* November 1993.

Lewis, William H., and Marks, Edward. *Triage for Failing States.* January 1994.

Maurer, Martha. *Coalition Command and Control.* 1994.

Quinn, Dennis J., ed. *Peace Support Operations and the U.S. Military.* 1994.

APPENDIX B:
Humanitarian Relief
Organizations Active in Somalia

CRS   Catholic Relief Services—Food and clothing distribution

IMC   International Medical Corps—Hospital support services

AWO   Abu Dabi Welfare Organization—Funds for food and clothing

DCG   Diakonic Care Germany—Assistance to children and orphans

CARE   CARE International—General relief services for displaced people

ADRA   Adventist Relief and Development Agrncy—Aid in local schools, etc.

AMA   Africa Muslims Agency—General welfare support services

COSV   Coordination Committee of Organizations for Voluntary Service—General management and supervision services

AICF   International Action Against Famine—Emergency food relief service

SOS   Childrens Emergency Services—Care and feeding for children

MERCY   Mercy International—First aid and

	related assistance
MSF	Doctors Without Frontiers—Triage support for illness and trauma wounds
MCF	Muwafaq Charity Foundation—Private Islamic group providing food and clothing
PSF	Pharmacists Without Borders —Provides essential pharmacology
RIHS	Revival Islamic Heritage Society—Religious support services
SCR	Swedish Church Relief—General food and clothing aid
NORCROSS	Nordic Red Cross—Provide emergency shelter and food
ICRC	International Committee of the Red Cross—Observer Status
FRCS	Federation of the Red Cross Society—general coordination
OXFAM	Oxford Famine Relief—U.K. food relief organization
CWS	Church World Services—Provide food and clothing
ACORD	Agency for Cooperation and Research Devlopment—Coordination of planning for infrastructure and insititution building
AFSC	American Friends Service Committee—Emergency clothing and feeding
IARA	Islamic African Relief Agency—Aid to indigent Muslims
IIRO	International Islamic Relief

	Organization—Food and clothing services
IDRA	International Development and Relief Agency—Coordinate relief efforts on part of various international organizations
DAWA	Munzamai Islamic Society—Muslim relief in form of clothing, etc.
MAUK	Muslim Aid UK—Islamic support for needy displaced persons
SCF	Save the Children—U.K. and U.S. food and clothing relief aid
ACSSOM	African Charity Society for Maternity and Childhood—Maternity support program

United Nations Humanitarian Agencies

UNHCR	United Nations High Commissioner for Refugees
UNICEF	United Nations Childrens Fund
UNESCO	United Nations Educational and Scientific Organization
UNDP	United Nations Development Program
UNCTAD	United Nations Conference on Trade and Devlopment
ECOSOC	Economic and Social Council

APPENDIX C:
Missions and Tasks of the UNITAF Civil-Military Operations Center (CMOC)

Mission

The CMOC was the key coordinating point for Humanitarian Relief Organizations in their dealings with UNITAF.

Functions

1. Validation of requests for military support. This included requests within the Mogadishu area, long haul convoy, security escorts to the interior, and requests for support at specific sites within the UNITAF area of operations. Military support to HROs within a Humanitarian Relief Sector was usually the responsibility of the local military commander and his CMOC.

2. Coordination of requests for military support within the various military components of UNITAF.

3. Convening and hosting ad hoc mission planning groups as an arm of the UNITAF J-3, for requests involving complicated military support and/or numerous military units and HROs.

4. Promulgating and explaining UNITAF policies to

the humanitarian community.

5. Providing information on UNITAF operations and the general security situation via daily security briefings.

6. Administering and issuing HRO identification cards.

7. Validating HRO personnel requests for space-available seats on UNITAF aircraft.

8. Acting as an interface, facilitator and coordination agency between UNITAF elements and HROs and UNOSOM headquarters staff.

9. Chairing Mogadishu Port Shipping Committee which dealt with pier space, port access and related issues important to HROs.

10. Acting as the agency that retrieved and returned weapons confiscated from HRO organizations.

11. Responding to emergency requests for assistance from HROs in the Mogadishu area either by responding directly with CMOC assets. or by requesting assistance via the UNITAF Joint Operations Center (JOC).

12. Maintaining and operating a 24-hour watch in the CMOC.

13. Maintaining contact with regional CMOCs.

14. Supporting, as required, a six-person Civil Affairs Team.

15. Facilitating the creation of a Food Logistics System for Somalia which factored in food stocks, delivery dates, warehousing capacities, transport availability and road repair efforts to create a basic matrix for food relief efforts within the UNITAF area of operations.

Headquarters Structure

Rank	Billet
Command	
Colonel	Director
Lt. Colonel	Deputy Director
Operations	
Major	Operations/Civil Affairs Operations Officer
Captain (2)	Asst Operations Officer
MSgt	Operations Chief
SFC	Admin Chief
Sgt	Asst Admin Chief
Cpl and Below	Driver/Security/Clerk
Transport	
Major	Convoy/Control/ Transportation Officer
Captain	Asst Transportation Officer
SFC	Air NCO
Cpl	Driver/Security/Clerk

ABOUT THE AUTHOR

COL Kenneth Allard, U.S. Army, is Senior Military Fellow at the Institute for National Strategic Studies, National Defense University, and also serves as an Adjunct Professor in the National Security Studies Program at Georgetown University. Previously he was Special Assistant to the Chief of Staff of the Army from 1987-1990 after having worked on the 1986 DOD Reorganization (Goldwater-Nichols) Act as an Army Congressional Fellow. In addition to operational intelligence assignments in the United States and overseas, he has served on the faculty of the Social Sciences Department, United States Military Academy, and as Dean of Students at the National War College.

COL Allard has written extensively on information warfare, the military-technical revolution, and defense procurement reform. His most recent full-length-work, *Command, Control and the Common Defense* (Yale University Press, 1990), won the 1991 National Security Book Award and is included on the professional military reading list recommended by the Chairman of the Joint Chiefs of Staff.

COL Allard holds a Ph.D. from the Fletcher School of Law & Diplomacy and an MPA from Harvard University.